Quick Guide

MW01007243

This guide is c   e
shown together, v   e
mountains grouped   e
color-coded and thumb-indexed in the following manner.

BIRDS OF THE WILLAMETTE VALLEY REGION

By

Harry Nehls
Tom Aversa
Hal Opperman

R.W. Morse Company
Olympia, Washington

For Ken Batchelder (H.N.)

For Charlotte (T.A.)

For Anne and Lucien (H.O.)

Published by the R.W. Morse Company, Olympia, Washington
Copyright ©2004 by the R.W. Morse Company

Library of Congress Control Number: 2004106502
ISBN 0-9640810-4-0   **$14.95 Softcover**
First Edition 2004

Printed by
  Mantec Production Company, Hong Kong

Authors
  Harry Nehls, Tom Aversa, and Hal Opperman

Editor
  Hal Opperman

Cover and Interior Design
  Gina Calle, CrespoCompany.com

Map
  Shawn K. Morse

Bird Drawings
  Eric Kraig

Cover Photograph of Acorn Woodpecker
  Tom Munson

Contents

Common Local Birds

Here are some of the most common birds in the Willamette Valley Region. For more information about each bird, go to its Species Account.

Double-crested Cormorant
p. 81

Canada Goose
p. 31

Mallard
p. 41

Great Blue Heron
p. 85

Red-tailed Hawk
p. 107

Glaucous-winged Gull
p. 161

American Crow
p. 235

Rock Pigeon
p. 167

Northern Flicker
p. 203

Rufous Hummingbird
p. 191

Steller's Jay
p. 231

Western Scrub-Jay
p. 233

Downy Woodpecker
p. 199

Barn Swallow
p. 251

Violet-green Swallow
p. 245

Chestnut-backed
Chickadee

Black-capped
Chickadee

Red-breasted
Nuthatch

Bushtit

Bewick's
Wren

American
Robin

Spotted
Towhee

European
Starling

Song Sparrow p. 331

House Finch p. 361

Red-winged Blackbird p. 347

Dark-eyed Junco p. 341

American Goldfinch p. 369

Pine Siskin p. 365

House Sparrow p. 373

Introduction

Bird watching, or birding, has become one of America's most popular outdoor activities. It is estimated that one-fifth of all Americans — 46 million people — either watch or feed birds. Birding can be great family entertainment. It is easy to get started, inexpensive, healthy, and allows us to understand and appreciate the natural world.

Given the popularity of bird watching and the beauty of the Pacific Northwest, it is little wonder that the people of the Willamette Valley Region enjoy seeing and studying our local birds. The Region has a rich variety of bird life with over 200 species of birds that are permanent residents or regular annual visitors. These are the birds featured in this guide. Those readily found in the lowlands receive full Species Accounts. An additional 12 species likely to be encountered at higher elevations of the Cascade Range are illustrated and briefly discussed in a special section on Mountain Specialties.

Birds of the Willamette Valley Region is for beginning bird watchers who wish to identify the birds of the greater Willamette Valley area. This guide will also appeal to experienced birders who wish to learn more about the behavior, habitats, and seasonal occurrence of our local birds.

Our web site, at www.birdsofwillamettevalley.com, provides a synopsis of the guide and a method for ordering an autographed copy of the book. Corrections to the text will be posted here periodically. We openly solicit suggestions to make the guide more accurate and complete. Please send these to bobmorse@rwmorsecompany.com.

Geographical Coverage

The Willamette Valley is the largest drainage basin in Oregon, bordered by the crest of the Cascade Range on the east, the Calapooya Divide on the south, the Coast Range on the west, and the Columbia River on the north. Elevations range from tidewater at the mouth of the

Willamette River in Portland to above 11,000 feet in the Cascades. *Birds of the Willamette Valley Region* embraces ten Oregon counties: Multnomah, Columbia, Washington, Yamhill, Clackamas, Polk, Marion, Benton, Linn, and all but the coastal slope of Lane. It also covers three counties in neighboring Washington — Clark, Cowlitz, and the western half of Skamania — that share a similar topography, vegetation, and climate with the Willamette Valley. This book is for anyone interested in bird life in or near Portland-Vancouver, Longview, Salem, Corvallis, and Eugene. The term "Region", as used in the guide, refers to this entire geographic area, as depicted on the map inside the front cover.

CONSERVATION

The Willamette Valley offers a landscape of great beauty and natural diversity, yet at the same time it holds most of Oregon's human population and is the economic engine of the state. Intensive development of agriculture, forestry, manufacturing, and shipping, and the continued growth of urban and rural communities, have led to changes in habitat and habitat loss that impact our local bird populations. Pollution of the Region's streams from farms, pulp mills, sewage, marinas, garbage dumps, storm runoff, and myriad other sources has had a direct effect on the Region's waterbirds. Deforestation has also taken its toll, as have changing agricultural practices and urban and suburban sprawl. A diverse and thriving bird life is an excellent indicator of a healthy environment. Those who enjoy birds should do all they can to protect birds and their habitats. We urge you to support some of the many conservation organizations such as local Audubon chapters, the Wetlands Conservancy, the Tualatin Riverkeepers, the McKenzie River Trust, or The Nature Conservancy of Oregon, that strive to address and improve environmental conditions.

Identifying Birds

It can be confusing when you first start trying to identify birds. First, look at the general form, size, and color of the bird, and the length and shape of its bill. Check the Common Local Birds (pages vii-x) and see if it is there. If not, scan through the Species Account pages for your bird. Read the description — especially the **boldfaced** text — to see how it matches your bird. Compare range, similar species, and habitat. Keep comparing the bird to the book until you have a match.

Usually the best way to clinch an identification is by observing the different colors of a bird's feathering ("plumage") and bare parts (bill, legs, feet). Most of the plumages and color patterns for each bird species are unique. However, plumages may vary within the same species between the sexes, between adults and younger birds, and by season.

In some species the male and the female have distinctly different plumages. Good examples are Mallard, House Finch, Red-winged Blackbird, and Rufous Hummingbird . Usually the males have the most brilliant colors, as in these examples, while the females have muted colors so they are not easily detected as they incubate eggs and raise young. Other species such as Rock Pigeon, Steller's Jay, American Crow, and Song Sparrow show no plumage differences between the sexes.

Most birds seen in the Willamette Valley Region in spring and summer display what is known as their summer or "breeding" plumage. Birds seen here in winter are usually in their "non-breeding" or winter plumage. Typically, but not always, the breeding plumage is more colorful or highly patterned and the non-breeding plumage is more muted.

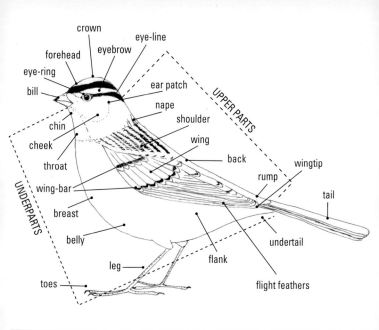

Parts of a Bird. It is helpful to know the names of the different parts of a bird. These sketches of a White-crowned Sparrow and an in-flight Mallard show the terms used to describe bird anatomy in this guide.

Molting is the process of replacing worn feathers with new, fresh feathers. Most local birds replace some or all of their feathers in a molt in summer or early fall when they change into their non-breeding plumage. Most birds molt again in late winter or spring as they change into their breeding plumage. These molts occur over a period of several weeks or months.

Some birds have different plumages as they mature. This is particularly true for gulls, which take up to four years and

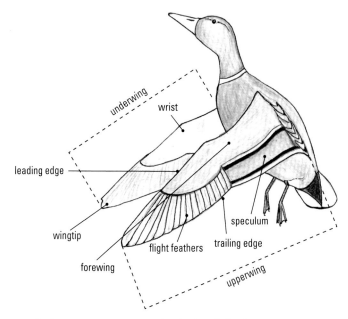

underwing

wrist

leading edge

wingtip

forewing

flight feathers

trailing edge

upperwing

speculum

several plumage stages to gain their adult plumage.

The term "juvenal plumage" refers to the plumage of a new-born bird after it loses its initial downy feathers. Some species hold this plumage for only a few weeks after fledging while others may hold it into winter. "First-year plumage" is used for the plumage during the first 12 months of a bird's life. "Immature" refers to all plumages before the bird gains its adult plumage.

Colors and patterning may vary considerably among birds of the same species and plumage stage, especially when they belong to different geographical populations. For instance, the Fox Sparrows that nest in the Cascades differ markedly in appearance from the ones that arrive to spend the winter in the lowlands of the Willamette Valley Region. Differences can be great even within the same local population. In our Region the majority of Red-tailed Hawks have light breasts and underwings, yet a certain percentage of birds have dark-brown underparts and dark underwings with lighter-colored flight feathers. Such consistently different types are called "color morphs" (or just morphs).

Don't expect every bird you see to look exactly like the photographs in this guide. Birds, like people, are individuals. To appreciate how variable birds of the same species can be, study the ones that come regularly to your backyard feeder. Male House Finches, for example, can show a wide range of coloration from rich, deep red to golden yellow. You may find that, with practice, you can learn to recognize individual birds by the subtle differences in their markings.

Binoculars

Binoculars are a great help in getting good views of birds. Binoculars come in many sizes. Each is labeled with two numbers, e.g., 7 x 35, 8 x 40, 10 x 50. The first number is the magnification. You may think that the larger the magnification, the better the binocular. However, as magnification increases, clarity may diminish as well as field of view (the width of the area you can see at a given distance). Another trade-off is that the higher-powered binoculars are usually heavier, hence harder to hold steady or carry for extended periods of time.

The second number is the diameter of the big lens (objective) in millimeters. The larger the diameter, the greater the light-gathering capability of the binocular and the more colors and details you can see, especially in poor light conditions.

Many discount stores offer binoculars in the $50 to $100 price range, which may be suitable for beginning birders. Higher-quality binoculars are available at nature stores or camera shops and can cost from $200 to $1500.

The best way to select a binocular is to go to a store that offers a range of models and try out several. If you wear glasses, fold, screw, or snap down the eyecups to get your pupil closer to the lens so you get a larger image. Look at a sign at the other end of the store and see which binocular provides the sharpest image. There should be no distortion in either shape or color. Which one feels more comfortable in the hand? Is it easy to change focus? Can you focus on close objects (within 10–15 feet)? Which is the most durable and has the largest field of view?

Out in the field, examine what other birders are using and ask for the opportunity to look through their binoculars. Selecting a binocular is a personal thing — what is comfortable for you may not be for another birder. So, choose one that has sufficient magnification (7 or 8 power), a wide objective lens (40 mm or more), an acceptable field of view (300 feet or more at 1000 yards), is easy to use, and fits your budget. A good rule of thumb is to buy the best binocular you can afford.

Also, make sure you get a wide binocular strap (at least one inch). It will help prevent a sore neck by the end of the day. Even better are some of the harnesses that transfer binocular weight to the shoulders rather than the neck. Binoculars also come with dust covers for each of the four lenses. Better-quality binoculars are waterproof, but in the Willamette Valley Region it is nonetheless a good idea to purchase a removable rain guard to cover the small eyepieces so you do not have to wipe them dry all the time.

Finally, take time to pre-focus your binocular before using it. Do this by adjusting the central focus knob and the eyepiece focus until the image appears sharp through both lenses.

Attracting Birds to Your Yard

Most people get involved in bird watching by observing the birds that appear in their yards. Perhaps the easiest way to see birds is to put up feeders and watch for birds to appear. When they are perched and eating, birds tend to stay long enough for you to study the field marks at close range and identify the bird.

Although just hanging out a birdseed feeder will attract some birds, a complete backyard bird program has three important requirements: **food**, **water**, and **shelter**. By careful attention to all three of these elements you will not only increase the number and variety of birds that visit your yard, but you will also be contributing to their wellbeing. Many helpful books and brochures on bird feeding, nest boxes, and gardening for wildlife are available at nature stores and nurseries.

FOOD

The food that birds eat comes mainly from natural sources. Native and ornamental shrubs, trees, and other plants provide fruits, seeds, flowers, and insects. You will attract more birds to your yard by selecting plants favorable to birds.

You may also provide seed, suet, and other products to entice birds to your yard. Many seeds are suitable for feeding birds although the best product in the Willamette Valley Region is black-oil sunflower seed, which has high oil and fat content. Many grocery and hardware stores sell a birdseed mix that contains some black-oil sunflower seed but often has a lot of millet (the small, round, tan-colored seed) and filler grains. When you place this seed in a hanging feeder five to six feet off the ground, some of the birds will eat only the sunflower seed and kick the filler and millet to the ground. In elevated feeders, it is much better to use only black-oil sunflower seed or a specialized mix that is high in nutritional value.

Different birds have different feeding preferences. You may wish to try more than one of the following common feeder types, depending on the species of birds you wish to attract.

- **Fly-through and hopper feeders** are hung or mounted on a pole or deck normally five to six feet above the ground. Stocked with black-oil sunflower seed, they attract jays, finches, nuthatches, and chickadees.

- A **ground feeder or platform feeder** is placed near the ground or up to table height and filled with millet, corn, or a birdseed mix that has some black-oil sunflower seeds but is mostly millet. This feeder will attract doves, pigeons, ducks, sparrows, Dark-eyed Junco, Spotted Towhee, and Red-winged Blackbird. Buy a ground feeder with a bottom screen that allows the rain to drain through.

- Cylindrical **tube feeders** are either hung or mounted and can be filled with a nutritional mix of birdseed or just black-oil sunflower seed. They attract the smaller birds such as Red-breasted Nuthatch, Pine Siskin, chickadees, and finches.

- A specialized tube feeder to hold niger thistle seed is called a **thistle or finch feeder** and can attract numbers of finches like House Finch, Pine Siskin, and American Goldfinch.

- **Suet**, either acquired at a local meat market or purchased at the nature store in suet cakes, attracts woodpeckers, Red-breasted Nuthatch, chickadees, Bushtit, and a host of other birds seeking its high-energy fat.

- Red **hummingbird feeders** attract Rufous and Anna's Hummingbirds that breed in the Willamette Valley Region. It is easy to make hummingbird nectar: mix one part sugar to four parts water, boil, let cool, and then fill your feeders. Do not add any artificial food coloring; the red of the feeder is sufficient to attract hummingbirds.

Experiment with your feeder locations and different birdseed to learn what works best in your yard. Feeders should be placed close to natural shelters such as bushes and trees so the birds can escape from predators. You can feed the birds all year long without worrying that your bird feeding will delay the birds' fall migration. They will leave when the time is right.

WATER

Birds need water for bathing and drinking. You will find that you attract more birds if you offer a reliable source of clean water in your yard. Consider placing a concrete birdbath filled with one inch of water to meet their needs. Clean and refill it regularly. Be sure the bottom surface is rough so the birds can get a good footing. Place the birdbath near shrubs or trees where they can preen after bathing and escape from predators. Try adding a dripper to the birdbath. The sound of dripping water attracts birds.

SHELTER AND NEST BOXES

Birds need cover so they can seek protection from bad weather and predators. Nearby bushes, shrubs, and trees will help meet their needs as will a loosely stacked brush pile. Neighborhood cats can be a real problem, especially when they lurk beneath feeders and birdbaths. Careful placement or screening off of feeders and birdbaths, or placing chicken wire strategically in front of favorite cat stalking areas, will help protect the birds.

Some of the birds featured in this guide are cavity nesters and may be enticed to use a bird house which you can either build yourself or purchase at a nature store. It is important to realize that there is no such thing as a generic nest box. Different birds have different needs, and each nest box has to meet the demands of its occupant or it will not be used. The size of the opening and its height above the floor are critical, as is the height of the nest box above the ground. Some nest boxes also serve as winter roosting boxes for the smaller birds. It may take a season or two to attract chickadees, nuthatches, or swallows to your nest boxes. Once they start nesting on your property, you will enjoy watching the behavior of these nesting birds.

HYGIENE

Feeders, the ground below the feeders, and birdbaths need to be cleaned on a regular basis to eliminate the possibility of the spread of avian diseases. Scrub the feeders and birdbaths with soap and water. Mix one part bleach to ten parts hot water to sanitize them. Rinse them well then let them dry completely before refilling.

Be sure to inspect nest boxes each fall and give them a good cleaning, but use no insecticides. Repair any damage so the boxes are ready and waiting for their new occupants to arrive in spring.

Observing Birds

Many bird watchers are quite content just to watch the birds in their yards casually. Some, however, get more involved and begin to look for birds beyond their immediate neighborhood. To get the most out of birding in the field, look, listen, and move slowly. Try to keep conversations to a minimum.

To help locate birds, watch for their movement and listen for their calls. Most often we see birds fly to a nearby branch or flit around in a tree. Their movement catches our attention. But an important part of bird watching is listening and, many times, it is its song or call that draws us to the bird.

Bird songs are a good way to identify birds. Each bird species has a unique song, and, with practice, you can learn to differentiate the songs. You can purchase tapes or CDs that allow you to study bird vocalizations at your leisure. With experience, you will be able to identify birds simply by their songs and calls.

When to Go Birding

Small birds tend to be most active when they are feeding early in the morning (as early as daybreak). Shorebirds tend to be most active while they are feeding on exposed mud around ponds and other water bodies, so water level is an important factor. Hawks become active in the morning after the rising temperature creates thermals that allow them to soar through the air. Most owls are nocturnal and are most active in the evening or just before dawn.

Willamette Valley birds vary with the season. If you go out in different seasons, you may see different birds. Some species stay in the Region throughout the year while others arrive in the spring and leave in the fall. Other species migrate into the lowlands of our area from the north, the mountains, or the interior of the continent and spend the winter.

Spring is a great time of year. The flowers are blossoming, the trees are getting their buds, and the birds, in their bright breeding plumages, return from their wintering grounds. The males start singing and the local nesting birds seek mates, breed, and start to raise their families. Hummingbirds feed on flower nectar or at feeders. Wintering birds head north to their breeding grounds.

In summer, the local young birds hatch, and their parents are busy feeding them. As summer progresses, the young learn to fly and fend for themselves. By August, summer visitors are beginning to head south for their wintering grounds.

By late fall, the last Arctic-breeding shorebirds have passed through on their way south. As fall changes to winter, flocks of waterfowl appear on our lakes and ponds. Dunlins arrive to winter on local fields and mudflats. Our resident birds continue to use neighborhood bird feeders, joined by winter visitors driven down to the lowlands by snowfall in the mountains.

KEEPING RECORDS

Some people keep a checklist of all the birds that appear in their yard ("yard list") or of all the birds seen in their lifetime ("life list"). As lists grow, so does a sense of personal accomplishment. Along with the pleasure of finding new and different birds comes an incentive to learn more about them. Many dedicated bird watchers keep a detailed journal of what they see, when and where, and the birds' behaviors. Careful record keeping by knowledgeable observers can contribute greatly to scientific understanding of bird life.

A checklist of the local birds is provided on pages 385–389.

Bird Habitats in the Willamette Valley Region

The place where a bird or other living creature is normally found is termed its "habitat". Birds are quite diverse in their habitat requirements. Brown Creepers are seldom seen over open water, or loons in trees. To a large extent, the secret to finding and identifying birds is knowing the habitats and developing an understanding of which birds are likely to be seen where. The more types of habitat you explore, the greater the variety of birds you will see.

The Willamette Valley Region has eleven major habitat categories:

GRASSLANDS

Extensive grasslands occur over much of the central valley, with a scattering of isolated oak trees. Flocks of Trumpeter and Tundra Swans, American Pipits, and Horned Larks are found here in winter, along with Northern Harriers and Rough-legged Hawks. Horned Lark, Savannah Sparrow, and Western Meadowlark are regular nesting species.

FARMLANDS

Much of the Willamette Valley and surrounding foothills has been converted to agricultural uses, including orchards, nurseries, and grass-seed production. Many fields are regularly plowed, some are burned, and others are left fallow. This provides a rich variety of habitats for wintering ducks, geese, starlings, and blackbirds. Large flocks of Killdeer winter in the fields, while Mourning Doves, California Quail, Ring-necked Pheasants, and Vesper Sparrows nest here.

HEDGEROWS AND BRUSHLANDS

Long rows of brushy hedges line many roadways and farm-field edges. Fallow fields often turn into extensive brush and berry tangles. Clearcuts and open areas at higher elevations are often covered with dense stands of *Ceanothus* and other shrubby plants. House Finches, White-crowned and Song Sparrows, Spotted Towhees, Lazuli Buntings, and Orange-crowned Warblers nest here. Large flocks of Golden-crowned and other sparrows occur in winter. At higher elevations, Nashville and MacGillivray's Warblers and Fox Sparrows are found in summer.

DECIDUOUS WOODLANDS

Low buttes and ridges, as well as other dry, less productive terrain in the valleys and foothills, are covered with stands of oaks, maples, and other deciduous trees, usually with a thick understory of brush and blackberry tangles. This habitat hosts a great number of nesting species, including Western Bluebird, House Wren, Hutton's, Warbling, and Red-eyed Vireos, Black-throated Gray and Wilson's Warblers, and many hawks and owls. Streamsides in the Cascade and Coast Ranges — much dryer than valley bottomlands — have species similar to those of the deciduous woodland habitat.

WOODED WET BOTTOM LANDS

The Willamette Valley floor has numerous sluggish streams and extensive bottomlands that are often flooded. Stands of cottonwood, ash, willow, and alder grow to large size here; many areas are quite boggy and can correctly be called swampy. Wood Duck, Hooded Merganser, Song Sparrow,

Yellow Warbler, Bewick's Wren, Black-capped Chickadee, and Downy Woodpecker are some of the expected species.

WETLANDS

Many of the numerous ponds, lakes, reservoirs, and streambeds in the Willamette Valley Region are edged with cattails and other marsh plants. Marshlands are valued; the most extensive are on state and federal refuges, carefully maintained to favor wildlife. Here can be found Virginia Rail, Sora, Marsh Wren, Common Yellowthroat, Red-winged and Yellow-headed Blackbirds, Double-crested Cormorant, waterfowl, and many other waterbird species. If left unmanaged, however, marshlands usually convert to dense, unproductive stands of invasive reed canary grass. Bogs and wet meadows in the Cascades provide nesting sites for Sandhill Cranes and Lincoln's Sparrows.

MUDFLATS

Late summer drawdown of most lakes and reservoirs provides mudflats and shallow water for migrating shorebirds and large waders. The Columbia and lower Willamette Rivers are tidal, with large flats often exposed at low tide. Ducks, geese, Sandhill Cranes, and American Pipits take advantage of this ephemeral habitat, as do great swarms of shorebirds.

LARGE WATER BODIES

Loons, diving ducks, and coots frequent deep, open waters of lakes, reservoirs, and wide rivers, along with Ospreys and Caspian Terns. Belted Kingfishers, Bald Eagles, gulls, and Great Blue Herons forage in the shallows or along shorelines. Swallows and Black Terns skim the open waters, plucking food from the surface or flying insects from the air.

CONIFEROUS FORESTS

Some 70 percent of the Willamette Valley Region is covered by conifer forests. At low and middle elevations, Douglas-fir, western hemlock, and western redcedar are the dominant species. These woods are home to Band-tailed Pigeon, a few owls, Hairy Woodpecker, Hammond's Flycatcher, Steller's Jay, Chestnut-backed Chickadee, Winter Wren, Golden-crowned Kinglet, Varied Thrush, Western Tanager, Yellow-rumped Warbler, and Pine Siskin. At higher elevations, forests of silver fir, mountain hemlock, and subalpine fir host Blue Grouse, Gray Jay, Hermit Thrush, and Townsend's Warbler.

SUBALPINE PARKLAND AND ALPINE MEADOWS

This high-elevation, open habitat of the Cascades consists of meadows with alpine wildflowers and scattered stands of trees, up to the edge of mountain snowfields. Look here for Mountain Bluebird, American Pipit, Mountain Chickadee, Gray Jay, Clark's Nutcracker, Townsend's Solitaire, and Gray-crowned Rosy-Finch.

CITIES AND SUBURBS

Residential neighborhoods and city parks provide habitat for numerous species well-known to city dwellers. Rufous and Anna's Hummingbirds, House Finch, Pine Siskin, goldfinches, woodpeckers, chickadees, Red-breasted Nuthatch, and grosbeaks often come to backyard feeders. Rock Pigeon, American Crow, American Robin, European Starling, and House Sparrow are more at home in cities and suburbs than elsewhere. During the winter months Cooper's and Sharp-shinned Hawks and Merlins patrol the streets and bird feeders. Several pairs of Peregrine Falcons call mid-town Portland home.

Birding Around the Willamette Valley

After studying the birds in your yard, visit local parks and greenbelts. A selection of top birding locations is given below. For maps and directions to these and other fine Regional birding spots, consult the guides and web sites listed on pages 21-22.

Columbia River From the Gorge to Longview, the lowlands on both sides of the river are prime wintering areas for waterfowl and a host of other species. In Washington, key sites include the Woodland Bottoms, Ridgefield National Wildlife Refuge, the Vancouver Lake bottomlands, and Steigerwald Lake National Wildlife Refuge. On the Oregon side, the Scappoose Bottoms, Sauvie Island, Smith/Bybee Lakes, the Vanport Wetlands, and the Sandy River delta are of particular importance.

Metropolitan Portland Numerous parks and natural areas are scattered in and around the city, from the lower Willamette Valley up onto the forested eastern slopes of the Coast Range. Forest Park, Mount Tabor Park, Oaks Bottom, Westmoreland Park, and Crystal Springs in Eastmoreland Park are among the best for birding. The Tualatin Valley is especially rich, with many prime bird-watching sites set aside, including the Killin Wetlands near Banks, Scoggins Valley Park, the Fernhill Wetlands, and Jackson Bottom.

Salem Brushlands in Minto-Brown Park attract many birds. Extensive wetlands at Baskett Slough National Wildlife Refuge, and surrounding farmlands, provide habitat for nesting and wintering waterfowl, hawks, and shorebirds. The nature trail through the oak grove to Baskett Butte offers good upland birding. Ankeny National Wildlife Refuge has open meadows, many hedges, vegetated streambanks, and several good nature trails.

Corvallis The E.E. Wilson Wildlife Area contains extensive brushy habitat with ponds and wetlands. Finley National Wildlife Refuge and surrounding farmlands attract large populations of wintering waterfowl. The refuge woodlands hold many upland species. Between the towns of Tangent and Harrisburg is the largest grassland prairie in the Willamette Valley. Reservoirs on the Santiam River near Sweet Home are good bets for waterbirds and woodland birds.

Eugene The foothills of the Cascades and Calapooya Mountains cover much of the south end of the Willamette Valley. Spencer Butte in Eugene is one of the better birding spots. Several reservoirs on the upper Willamette River are worth visiting. Perhaps the best birding site in the Willamette Valley is Fern Ridge Reservoir. The Fern Ridge Wildlife Area at the south end of the lake provides marshes, mudflats, and wetlands. Nearby brush and hedges shelter upland birds. Many species more regular east of the Cascades, such as Western and Clark's Grebes, nest about the lake.

Cascade Range Roads and trails on the west slopes of the Cascades provide excellent conifer-forest birding and access to many lakes and reservoirs, among them Timothy Lake. The Santiam Pass area is especially good; highways from Salem, Corvallis, and Eugene converge here. The Three Sisters and Mount Jefferson Wilderness Areas include extensive subalpine and alpine habitats, but hard work is required to visit them. Timberline Lodge gives good access to the alpine zone on Mount Hood and is easily reached by automobile. In the southwestern Washington Cascades, various approaches to Mount Saint Helens offer fine, accessible forest birding.

Helpful Resources

There are a number of ways to get additional information about birds and their habitats, bird identification, and good places to go birding. Some of the best information is available through books, birding organizations, web sites, and local nature stores. Here are some of our favorites:

REGIONAL PUBLICATIONS

Joseph E. Evanich, Jr. 1990. *The Birder's Guide to Oregon*. Portland Audubon Society. Maps, descriptions, directions; includes the Region's most important birding sites.

John Fitchen. 2004. *Birding Portland and Multnomah County*. Eugene: Oregon Field Ornithologists.

Michael Houck and M.J. Cody (eds.). 2000. *Wild in the City: A Guide to Portland's Natural Areas*. Portland: Oregon Historical Society. Maps, descriptions of all major natural areas in Metropolitan Portland-Vancouver; most are excellent for birding.

Susan Peter, Shirley Ewart, and Barbara Schaffner. 2002. *Exploring the Tualatin River Basin*. Corvallis: Oregon State University Press. Maps, directions, descriptions of 85 natural areas.

David B. Marshall, Matthew G. Hunter, and Alan L. Contreras (eds.). 2003. *Birds of Oregon: A General Reference*. Corvallis: Oregon State University Press. Detailed accounts of every species recorded in state. Standard reference for status, distribution, natural history.

Hal Opperman. 2003. *A Birder's Guide to Washington*. With contributions from members of the Washington Ornithological Society. Colorado Springs: American Birding Association. Includes maps, directions for more than 40 birding sites in interior southwestern Washington.

IDENTIFICATION GUIDES

David Allen Sibley. 2003. *The Sibley Field Guide to Birds of Western North America*. New York: Alfred A. Knopf.

Field Guide to the Birds of North America, 4th ed. 2002. Washington, D.C.: National Geographic Society.

Kenn Kaufman. 2000. *Birds of North America*. New York: Houghton Mifflin.

Roger Tory Peterson. 1990. *A Field Guide to Western Birds*, 3rd ed. Boston: Houghton Mifflin.

OTHER REGIONAL BIRDING RESOURCES

There are five local *Audubon Society* chapters in the Willamette Valley Region. For information about each, and local birding news, visit them on the Internet:

Audubon Society of Corvallis	www.audubon.corvallis.or.us
Audubon Society of Portland	www.audubonportland.org
Lane County Audubon Society	www.laneaudubon.org
Salem Audubon Society	www.salem-audubon.org
Vancouver Audubon Society	www.vancouveraudubon.org

Oregon Birders On-Line (OBOL) is an e-mail list on birds and birding sponsored by Oregon State University — a lively forum and a good place to keep up with interesting bird sightings in the Region. Visit http://lists.oregonstate.edu/mailman/listinfo/obol for information on subscribing.

Oregon Field Ornithologists (OFO) is a statewide organization that leads field trips, publishes a quarterly journal and other publications, and holds annual conferences. The OFO web site, www.oregonbirds.org, offers information about the organization and its activities, a membership application, the latest state checklist, and a link to an on-line version of OBOL postings.

Nature Stores

The Audubon Society of Portland Nature Store, 5151 N.W. Cornell Road, Portland, OR 97210 (503-292-9453) has a fine selection of natural history items, books, seed, bird feeders, bird houses, and optics.

There are a number of good nature stores in the Willamette Valley Region. Their staffs are always eager to answer your bird and bird-feeding questions. The yellow pages of the telephone directory will locate the closest nature store.

Species Accounts

The following pages present accounts and photographs of the most familiar bird species of the Willamette Valley Region. Information on each species is presented in a standardized format: see the sample page (opposite) for an explanation. Species are grouped by families, color-coded and thumb-indexed. The Quick Guide on the first page inside the front cover of the book will help you locate the birds. A dozen species found mostly in the mountains are presented separately at the end (pages 375-381).

The following terms are used to describe the relative abundance of each species and the likelihood of finding it in a particular season. These definitions were developed by the American Birding Association.

- **Common:** Found in moderate to large numbers, and easily found in appropriate habitat at the right time of year.
- **Fairly Common:** Found in small to moderate numbers, and usually easy to find in appropriate habitat at the right time of year.
- **Uncommon:** Found in small numbers, and usually — but not always — found with some effort in appropriate habitat at the right time of year.
- **Rare:** Occurs annually in very small numbers. Not to be expected on any given day, but may be found with extended effort over the course of the appropriate season(s).

Birds shown in the photographs in the Species Accounts are adults unless the captions indicate otherwise.

NAME OF THE SPECIES
Its Latin name

Description: Length (and wingspan for larger species), followed by a description that includes differences in plumages between sexes and ages. Key field marks — unique markings visible in the field that help distinguish one species from another — are shown in **boldfaced** type.

Similar Species: Identifies similar-appearing species and describes how to tell them apart.

Seasonal Abundance: Identifies the times of year that the species is here and its relative abundance (see facing page for definitions of abundance terms). Also describes its overall range.

Where to Find: Explains generally where this bird may be found in the Willamette Valley Region; may also suggest some of the better locations to search for it.

Habitat: Describes the habitat(s) in which this bird is normally found in the Willamette Valley Region.

Diet and Behavior: Identifies the prime sources of food and highlights behaviors characteristic of this species.

Voice: Describes the main song and calls of the species.

Did you know? Provides interesting facts about this species.

Date and Location Seen: A place for you to record the date and location of your first sighting of this species.

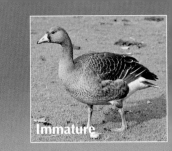
Immature

Description: 30″, wingspan 53″ (averages). Mostly brownish-gray; rump, lower belly, undertail white. **Tail dark with white tip.** ADULT: **White line between flank, folded wing. Front of face white**, variable black barring on belly; bill pink, **legs bright-yellow-orange**. IMMATURE: Lacks white face, flank line, dark belly patches; bill yellowish, legs paler than adult.

Similar Species: Canada Goose (page 31) with white cheek patch, dark bill, legs; dark tail lacks white tip.

Seasonal Abundance: Fairly common migrant, uncommon winter resident in Region, mid-August–May. Nests around northern hemisphere on Arctic tundra, wintering to tropics. Many migrate non-stop from Alaska to Klamath Basin, passing inland at mouth of Columbia River to continue southward over Willamette Valley.

Where to Find: Large flocks often heard flying overhead. Individuals, small groups join wintering Canada Goose flocks.

Habitat: Agricultural fields, wetlands.

Diet and Behavior: Gleans in fields for grain, grasses, potatoes, other root crops; grubs with head under water or tipping up for roots, rhizomes of aquatic plants. Highly gregarious, often joining other wild goose flocks, park or barnyard birds.

Voice: Sometimes called "laughing goose", for high-pitched, yelping *tal luk, to ha luk,* given constantly in flight.

Did you know? White-fronts are quite variable in size, depending on sex (males larger) and on geographic race.

Date and Location Seen: _____

Description: 28", wingspan 54". White goose with **black wingtips**, pinkish legs, **pink bill with blackish "grinning patch"**. JUVENILE: Dusky upperparts, grayish legs. Dark variant called Blue Goose (rare in Region) gray with white head, neck.

Similar Species: Swans larger without black wingtips. Ross's Goose (not shown; rare in Region) smaller with stubby bill.

Seasonal Abundance: Common but very local winter resident in Region, arrives October, departs by May. Breeds on Arctic tundra from northeastern Russia east to Greenland, winters to northern Mexico. Most birds wintering in Region come from Wrangel Island, Siberia.

Where to Find: Local wintering grounds limited to Sauvie Island, Ridgefield National Wildlife Refuge. Stragglers, migrants often seen among goose flocks throughout Willamette Valley.

Habitat: Short-grass or post-production agricultural fields.

Diet and Behavior: Forages mostly on land but also in shallow water, almost entirely on plant materials including grasses, shoots, waste grain. Highly gregarious. Noisy, single-species flocks often number 1,000 or more birds, filling sky when flushed.

Voice: Highly vocal. Raucous, high-pitched, honking yelps.

Did you know? Snow Geese are often called "wavies" due to the undulating, irregular waves they form in flight.

Date and Location Seen: _____

Cackling form (right)

Description: 35", wingspan 50" (averages). Mostly grayish-brown with black legs, bill, tail; white rump, undertail; **black head, neck, with white chin patch**. Small, dark, short-necked, highly migratory Cackling form (less common in Region) barely larger than Mallard.

Similar Species: Brant (not shown; rare migrant, winter visitor in Region) much darker, lacks white chin patch. Greater White-fronted Goose (page 27) has pink bill, yellow legs, lacks chin patch.

Seasonal Abundance: Common resident in Region. Migratory races arrive October, depart by May. Ranges throughout North America south to Texas, introduced in Europe, New Zealand.

Where to Find: Throughout lowlands, primarily at refuges. Ankeny National Wildlife Refuge best for Cackling.

Habitat: Ponds, lakes, marshes, grassy fields; less often, rivers.

Diet and Behavior: Forages mostly on land but also in water, primarily for plant materials including waste grains. Did not formerly breed in Region, but introduced populations have become habituated to humans, now thrive year round in urban areas, grazing on available lawns. Nests, unfazed, in close proximity to human activities.

Voice: Honk, although smaller races give higher-pitched yelping.

Did you know? Geese mate for life, unlike ducks. The female incubates while the male protects the nesting territory — hissing, pumping his head up and down, or rushing at intruders with neck held low.

Date and Location Seen: _____

Trumpeter Swan

Tundra Swan

TRUMPETER SWAN / TUNDRA SWAN
Cygnus buccinator / Cygnus columbianus

Description: 60" / 52", wingspan 80" / 66". Huge, white, **long-necked** waterfowl with black bill as adults, juvenile bill pinkish. TRUMPETER: Larger; long **black bill extends to eye in broad triangle**; juvenile retains gray plumage throughout spring. TUNDRA: Smaller; **bill tapers to thin horizontal line at eye**; usually patch of yellow skin below eye; **juvenile white by spring.**

Similar Species: Snow Goose (page 29) smaller, has black wingtips. Introduced Mute Swan (not shown) has orange bill with black knob at base.

Seasonal Abundance: TRUMPETER: Uncommon, local winter resident in Region, often mixed in Tundra flocks. Breeds south-central Alaska, other scattered locations in western North America. TUNDRA: Common winter resident in Region (November–March). Breeds on high-latitude tundra in Eurasia, North America, winters to temperate zone.

Where to Find: Lowlands. Trumpeter most likely on farm fields between Monmouth, Eugene.

Habitat: Ponds, marshes, agricultural fields.

Diet and Behavior: Forage on plant materials on land or in water, including waste grains, potatoes. Gregarious, often in flocks including both species; may roost on open water.

Voice: TRUMPETER: Lower-pitched, like trumpet. TUNDRA: Gooselike barking *klow wow*.

Did you know? The Trumpeter Swan, close to extinction a century ago, is rapidly recovering.

Date and Location Seen: _____

Male

Female

Description: 17", wingspan 30". Unique, short-necked duck, with long, broad tail, **swept-back crest**, white belly, dark-blue speculum bordered at rear by white. MALE: Spectacularly **multicolored**. Green head; white partial neck collar; face pattern; scarlet eye-ring, bill base. Dull in summer, retaining head pattern, red bill. FEMALE: Brownish with broad **teardrop-shaped eye-ring.**

Similar Species: Mandarin Duck (not shown; introduced from Asia, rare in Region). Male gaudy with white face, orange "side-whiskers"; females closely similar but Mandarin with lighter head, upperparts; eye-ring smaller.

Seasonal Abundance: Fairly common resident in Region, widespread in summer, flocking in winter (October–March). Ranges across U.S., southern Canada; winters to Mexico, Caribbean.

Where to Find: Lowlands to moderate elevations. Best bet Crystal Springs Lake (Portland).

Habitat: Wooded swamps, ponds; shady, slow rivers; rarely open lakes.

Diet and Behavior: Forages mostly in water, seldom upending. Diet mainly seeds; takes more insects in summer. Nests in cavities. Almost as likely to be seen on tree branches as in water.

Voice: Male gives thin, high whistles, female penetrating *ooo eeek* when flushed or alarmed.

Did you know? Threatened with extinction a century ago by over-hunting, Wood Ducks have recovered, aided in part by placement of thousands of nest boxes.

Date and Location Seen: _____

Male

Female

Description: 19", wingspan 33". Medium-sized, rather plain dabbling duck with **white belly**, steep forehead, yellow feet, **white patch in speculum**. MALE: Mostly plain, variegated gray with back plumes, puffy head shape, dark bill, **black rump, undertail**; dull as female in summer. FEMALE: Mottled brown with yellowish-orange on sides of bill.

Similar Species: Female Mallard (page 41) longer, more bulky, lacks white speculum.

Seasonal Abundance: Fairly common winter resident in Region, uncommon in summer. Ranges across North America, Eurasia in middle latitudes, winters to subtropics.

Where to Find: Throughout lowlands, especially on shallow ponds rich in aquatic vegetation.

Habitat: Ponds, lakes, marshes.

Diet and Behavior: Forages primarily for plant material, dabbling at surface, upending, or occasionally grazing on land. Sociable, often flocking with other dabblers. Pair formation begins by fall.

Voice: Male with unique, low-pitched *reb reb* call, also squeaky whistle. Female gives nasal quack.

Did you know? Gadwalls were historically present in much lower numbers in the Willamette Valley. They have increased dramatically in recent years.

Date and Location Seen: _____

Eurasian Wigeon
Male

American Wigeon
Male

American Wigeon
Female

Description: 19″, wingspan 32″. Short-necked dabbling ducks with **bluish-gray bill**, relatively long tail, **white forewing patch**. EURASIAN: **Gray sides**, white flanks, black undertail, **reddish head, yellowish forehead**. AMERICAN: Similar with **brownish sides, gray head, white forehead, green behind eye**. Females, summer males duller.

Similar Species: Gadwall (page 37) has white in speculum, not forewing; female has yellow on bill.

Seasonal Abundance: EURASIAN: Uncommon winter resident in Region, in flocks of Americans. Ranges across Eurasia, winters to tropics; some stray to North America. AMERICAN: Common winter resident in Region, arrives late August, departs by May; very rare breeder. Breeds across North America, winters to Central America.

Where to Find: Widespread in lowlands, regularly at city parks, golf courses such as Eastmoreland, Westmoreland Parks (Portland), Commonwealth Park (Beaverton).

Habitat: Ponds, marshes, flooded fields, short-grass fields.

Diet and Behavior: Mostly plant material. Graze more than other ducks. Forage in water by skimming surface, rarely upending; also steal plants from American Coots, diving ducks. Form large, tight flocks, especially on land.

Voice: Distinctive *wee whe whir* whistled by males, female with growling quack.

Did you know? Wigeons are called Baldpates by hunters.

Date and Location Seen: _____

Male

Female

Description: 22", wingspan 35". Large, **heavy-bodied** dabbling duck with orange legs, **blue speculum** bordered front, rear with white. MALE: Grayish sides with darker back, chestnut breast, white neck-ring, yellow bill, **iridescent-green head**; in summer dull as female. FEMALE: Mottled brown with blotchy yellowish bill.

Similar Species: In female-type plumage, told from other dabbling ducks by larger size, speculum pattern.

Seasonal Abundance: Common resident in Region; numbers augmented in winter with migrants from north. Ranges around northern hemisphere from subarctic to subtropics.

Where to Find: Widespread in Region, less common in mountains.

Habitat: Any body of water, agricultural fields, city parks.

Diet and Behavior: Forages in water — upending, skimming near surface, even diving (rarely), mostly for plant but also for animal material. Grazes on land for waste grain, grass, insects. In parks becomes habituated to humans, takes handouts. Strong flyer. Gregarious, often flocking with other ducks. Pair formation, courtship begin in fall, nesting as early as late March.

Voice: Female makes familiar quacking. Male offers single whistles while courting, grating calls in aggression.

Did you know? Mallards are the origin of every variety of domestic duck except the Muscovy.

Date and Location Seen: _____

Blue-winged Teal
Male

Blue-winged Teal
Female

Cinnamon Teal
Male

Description: 15", wingspan 23". Small dabblers with **long, dark bill**, green speculum, **powder-blue forewing patch visible in flight**. BLUE-WINGED: Male brown with white flank patch, head gray with **bold white crescent behind bill**; dull as female in summer. Female mottled brown with diffuse pale facial area behind bill. CINNAMON: Male **chestnut-red** with red eye; dull as female in summer. Female mottled brown with plain face. Nearly impossible to distinguish juvenile Blue-winged from Cinnamon Teal, but latter averages longer bill, plainer face.

Similar Species: Larger, longer-billed than Green-winged Teal (page 49).

Seasonal Abundance: BLUE-WINGED: Uncommon breeder in Region; much more common as early-May migrant. Ranges Alaska, Labrador south to Texas, winters south to Brazil. CINNAMON: Fairly common breeder, present in Region from March through November; rare in winter. Breeds western North America, winters south to Patagonia.

Where to Find: Mostly lowlands.

Habitat: Ponds, marshes, flooded fields.

Diet and Behavior: Both forage for plant, animal matter in shallows, rarely upending. Blue-winged eats more insects. Fast, agile fliers, frequently found in small groups of mixed species of teals.

Voice: Female quacks; male chatters, whistles.

Did you know? Closely related, Blue-winged and Cinnamon Teals hybridize rarely but regularly.

Date and Location Seen: _____

Male

Female

Description: 18″, wingspan 29″. Fairly small dabbling duck with **very large spoon-shaped bill**, green speculum, orange legs, **powder-blue forewing patch visible in flight**. MALE: White breast, **rust-brown belly, sides**; iridescent-green head, yellow eye, black bill. Dull as female in summer. FEMALE: Mottled brown with dark eye, orangish bill.

Similar Species: Bill size, shape distinctive.

Seasonal Abundance: Common winter, fairly common summer resident in Region; numbers augmented when migrants arrive in late summer. Ranges across northern temperate zone of Old, New Worlds, winters to tropics.

Where to Find: Widespread in lowlands, often abundant at sewage ponds.

Habitat: Ponds, lakes, marshes, flooded fields.

Diet and Behavior: Feeds while swimming, often in flocks in tight, circling masses. Forages by sweeping bill from side to side to skim, filter at surface for plant, animal matter, seldom upending. May mix with other ducks, but tends to flock with own species. Courting, pair formation begin late winter; males attain breeding plumage later than other dabblers.

Voice: Male gives low calls during courtship; female quacks hoarsely.

Did you know? Shovelers' filter-feeding is facilitated by lamellae — transverse ridges inside the edges of the upper and lower bill that act as sieves, trapping food particles.

Date and Location Seen: _____

Male

Female

Description: 20″ (male 26″ with tail), wingspan 33″. **Slender**, long-necked dabbling duck with long, thin bill, **green speculum** bordered with buff at front, white at rear. MALE: Grayish with brown head, long, needle-like tail, **white on breast extending in thin line up side of neck**; dull as female in summer. FEMALE: Mottled grayish-brown with short, pointed tail, **dark-gray bill**.

Similar Species: In female-type plumage, slender shape, dark bill separate from other dabblers.

Seasonal Abundance: Common winter resident in Region, rare breeder. Highly migratory with transients arriving by August, departing by April. Breeds from Arctic to middle latitudes in North America, Eurasia; winters to tropics.

Where to Find: Lowlands, especially Jackson Bottom (Hillsboro), Sauvie Island; less common near urbanized areas.

Habitat: Ponds, marshes, shallow lakes, flooded fields.

Diet and Behavior: Mostly dabbles in shallow water but may walk on land, foraging. Diet mainly plant material including waste grain, also takes insects, aquatic organisms. Gathers in large or small groups, often with other ducks.

Voice: Fairly vocal, male with fluty *toop toop*, also high, buzzy calls; female quacks.

Did you know? Northern Pintails nest, and migrate, earlier than most waterfowl. Some head north by late February and start back south as early as late June.

Date and Location Seen: _____

Male

Female

Description: 13", wingspan 23". **Small** dabbling duck with **short, dark bill, green speculum**. MALE: Grayish with red-and-green head, yellow undertail, **white vertical bar on side**; dull as female in summer. FEMALE: Mottled brown with dark line through eye.

Similar Species: Smaller, more compact, shorter-billed than other dabblers; female eye-line more pronounced.

Seasonal Abundance: Common winter resident in Region, rare breeder. Highly migratory with transients arriving by August, departing by May. Breeds from Arctic to middle latitudes in North America, Eurasia; winters to tropics.

Where to Find: Mostly lowlands, rarely in mountains.

Habitat: Ponds, marshes, shallow lakes, flooded fields.

Diet and Behavior: Forages by dabbling in shallow water or walking on wet mud, filtering water for plant materials, small aquatic organisms. Gathers in large or small groups, often with other ducks. Flocks fly swiftly in tight units, leaving water quickly, apparently with little effort. Courting, pair formation begin in winter.

Voice: Male highly vocal with ringing *peep*; female gives weak, nasal quack.

Did you know? The Eurasian race, called Common Teal and sometimes considered a separate species, is a rare winter visitor to the Willamette Valley Region. It is recognized by the horizontal instead of vertical white bar on the side.

Date and Location Seen: _____

Redhead Male

Male

Female

Description: 21", wingspan 29". Sleek, elegant, long-necked diving duck with **sloping forehead, long, dark bill**, plain grayish wings. MALE: Black at both ends with **whitish back, sides. Head, neck chestnut-reddish**; eye red. FEMALE: Browner overall, lacks red head, eye.

Similar Species: Distinctive head shape, plumage separate Canvasback from scaups (page 55). Male **Redhead** (see inset; rare in Region) distinguished by **head, bill shape, pattern; grayer back**.

Seasonal Abundance: Fairly common but local winter resident, arrives by October, most depart by April. Breeds in western North America from central Alaska to South Dakota, winters east to New England, south to Mexico.

Where to Find: Throughout lowlands. Best bets Fernhill Wetlands (Forest Grove), Jackson Bottom (Hillsboro).

Habitat: Lakes, ponds, sewage lagoons, marshes with open water.

Diet and Behavior: Dives, mostly in shallow water, primarily for plant materials; may also dabble, take aquatic insects. Sociable; gathers in flocks, often with other ducks. Courts less on wintering grounds than other ducks, as most pair formation occurs later in spring on migration.

Voice: Female grunts, male cooing sounds seldom heard in Region.

Did you know? The Canvasback's Latin species name, *valisineria*, refers to wild celery — an important food item.

Date and Location Seen: _____

Male

Female

RING-NECKED DUCK
Aythya collaris

Description: 17″, wingspan 24″. Short-necked diving duck with **peaked head, pale ring near tip of gray bill**, grayish wings in flight. MALE: Purplish-iridescent head, **black back**, breast; **vertical white mark on gray side** in front of wing. FEMALE: Brownish **with white eye-ring**, diffuse pale facial area near bill.

Similar Species: Lesser Scaup (page 55) head less peaked, no ring on bill; male with gray back, female with bold white face patch at bill base.

Seasonal Abundance: Common winter resident in Region, arrives by September, most depart by April; uncommon breeder. Nests northern North America from western Alaska to Labrador, winters to Central America, Caribbean.

Where to Find: Widespread in lowlands in migration, winter. Nests woodland ponds in Cascades, occasionally lowlands.

Habitat: Ponds, lakes, sewage lagoons, marshes.

Diet and Behavior: Mostly dives, but may also dabble in fairly shallow water. Diet aquatic plants, insects, snails, other invertebrates. Sociable. Flocks may be large or small, single-species or mixed with other divers on large water bodies; also flocks with dabblers on small ponds.

Voice: Male whistles, female growls softly.

Did you know? Unlike other diving ducks, Ring-necked Ducks are able to spring directly off the water into flight, allowing them to use small ponds surrounded by trees.

Date and Location Seen: _____

Greater Scaup
Female

Greater Scaup
Male

Lesser Scaup
Male

Description: 18" / 17", wingspan 28" / 26". Short-necked diving ducks with bluish-gray bill, **white wing stripe** visible in flight. MALES: **Blackish on both ends, whitish in middle**, head darkly iridescent. FEMALES: Brownish with **white facial patch at bill base**. GREATER: **Head round**, neck thicker, bill wider, male's head glosses greenish. LESSER: **Peaked crown**, neck thinner, bill smaller, **wing stripe extends only halfway to wingtip**, male's head glosses purplish.

Similar Species: Ring-necked Duck (page 53) head more peaked, ring near bill tip; male with black back, vertical white mark on side.

Seasonal Abundance: GREATER: Uncommon winter resident in Region; arrives by October, departs in May. Breeds around world in far north, winters to temperate zone. LESSER: Common winter resident in Region, rare in summer; arrives by October, most depart by April. Breeds western North America (Alaska to Colorado); winters south as far as Colombia.

Where to Find: Mostly lowlands. Best bets Columbia River, Fern Ridge Reservoir. Greaters usually found in flocks with Lessers.

Habitat: Lakes, sewage ponds, rivers.

Diet and Behavior: Dive for mollusks, other aquatic animals, plants. Highly gregarious, gathering in tight flocks, often including both scaup species, other ducks.

Voice: Grating sounds, deep whistles.

Did you know? Hunters refer to both species of scaups as Bluebills.

Date and Location Seen: _____

Male

Female

Description: 13", wingspan 20". **Small**, plump diving duck, with **small gray bill**, white belly, white wing patches easily visible in flight. MALE: Mostly white with dark back, iridescent-blackish **puffy head with white patch at back**. FEMALE: Dull grayish with **small, oval white cheek patch**, smaller wing patches than male.

Similar Species: Goldeneyes (page 59) larger, white patch of male below rather than behind eye. Hooded Merganser (page 61) male has rusty sides with black-and-white bars. Ruddy Duck (page 65) has larger bill, cheek patch.

Seasonal Abundance: Common winter resident in Region. Most arrive October, depart by May; rare in summer. Nests in interior from central Alaska to Québec, winters on both coasts from Aleutians, Maritimes south to Mexico.

Where to Find: Throughout lowlands.

Habitat: Lakes, ponds, marshes, flooded farm fields.

Diet and Behavior: Dives for insects, other aquatic organisms, plant materials. Usually in small groups, but large concentrations occur at favorable sites. Patters on surface with rapid wing-beats before flying.

Voice: Fairly quiet in winter quarters but soft, growling whistles, grunts occasionally given.

Did you know? Although Buffleheads frequent open situations in migration and winter, in the breeding season they use forested habitat adjacent to water, nesting in cavities — especially old flicker nests.

Date and Location Seen: _____

Common Goldeneye
Male

Common Goldeneye
Female

Barrow's Goldeneye
Male

Barrow's Goldeneye
Female

COMMON GOLDENEYE / BARROW'S GOLDENEYE
Bucephala clangula / Bucephala islandica

Description: 18", wingspan 27". Plump, short-necked, with short bill, **puffy head, white wing patch**. MALES: White with black-and-white back, dark iridescent head, white patch below eye. FEMALES: Grayish with brown head. COMMON: Head peaked in middle, male's **green with round patch**; less black on back. BARROW'S: Head peaked at front, **steep forehead**, bill smaller. Male's **head purplish, patch crescent-shaped**; less white on back.

Similar Species: Bufflehead (page 57) smaller, male's head patch behind rather than below eye.

Seasonal Abundance: COMMON: Fairly common winter resident in Region (October–April), rare in summer. Breeds across northern North America, Eurasia, winters to temperate zone. BARROW'S: Fairly common resident in Region in Cascades, rare in lowlands. Breeds Alaska south to Wyoming, Oregon, also northeastern Canada, Iceland; winters down both coasts in temperate zone.

Where to Find: COMMON: Widespread on larger lakes, rivers. BARROW'S: Mountain lakes, reservoirs. Best bet Lost Lake (Santiam Pass), in winter Foster Reservoir (Sweet Home).

Habitat: COMMON: Lakes, rivers, reservoirs. BARROW'S: Nests shallow mountain lakes, winters unfrozen lakes, rivers.

Diet and Behavior: Dive for aquatic animals, plants; form loose flocks outside nesting season. Nest in tree cavities; courting, displaying already by fall.

Voice: Soft grunts.

Did you know? Goldeneyes' wings create a loud whistling sound in flight.

Date and Location Seen: _____

Male

Female

Description: 16", wingspan 23". Small, **long-tailed** duck with thin, **saw-toothed bill**, conspicuous **puffy crest**, white belly. Small white wing patches visible in flight. MALE: Striking; mostly blackish above including bill, with fan-shaped white crest, rusty sides, black-and-white side bars, ornamental back plumes; dull as female in late summer. FEMALE: Brownish-gray with yellowish-edged bill.

Similar Species: Other mergansers (page 63) larger, with reddish bills. Bufflehead (page 57) female smaller with small cheek patch; male has white sides.

Seasonal Abundance: Fairly common resident in Region, less common in summer. Ranges across North America from southeastern Alaska, Oregon, to Great Lakes, New Brunswick; winters to California, southeastern states.

Where to Find: Mostly lowlands, rarely to higher elevations.

Habitat: Breeds at wooded ponds, sloughs, sluggish creeks with emergent vegetation, flocking in winter on more-open waters such as sewage ponds.

Diet and Behavior: Forages visually by diving, swimming underwater for fish, aquatic insects, other organisms. Usually in small groups, but may concentrate at favorable sites in fall. Often allows close approach, then patters along surface with rapid wing-beats, flies off. Nests in tree cavities, also nest boxes.

Voice: Fairly vocal with soft croaks.

Did you know? Hooded Mergansers are quite secretive in summer, not often seen even where regular.

Date and Location Seen: _____

Male

Female

Description: 24", wingspan 34". **Robust**, white-bellied diving duck, with thin, **reddish saw-toothed bill, shaggy crest**. Large **white wing patches** visible in flight. MALE: Body mostly white with dark-green head, dark back; dull as female in late summer. FEMALE: Gray with brown head, white chin.

Similar Species: Red-breasted Merganser (not shown; rare in Region) female very similar but less bulky, with neither distinct white throat nor abrupt line between light-gray body, brown head; bill thinner at base. Hooded Merganser (page 61) much smaller, bill not reddish.

Seasonal Abundance: Common resident in Region. Ranges across forested areas of northern hemisphere to southern edge of temperate zone.

Where to Find: Throughout Region, sea level to mountain passes. Concentrates in large flocks during winter on rivers, lakes, sewage ponds.

Habitat: Any type of water body.

Diet and Behavior: Forages visually by diving, swimming underwater, mostly for fish; young eat aquatic insects. Nests near water in tree cavities, mostly along major rivers, but also near clear lakes, mountain streams; may be loosely colonial.

Voice: Hoarse croaking notes.

Did you know? Common Mergansers tend to segregate by sex in winter, with males predominating in the Willamette Valley. In Europe this species is called Goosander.

Date and Location Seen: _____

Male Breeding

Female

Description: 15", wingspan 19". Compact, **large-headed, broad-billed** diving duck with **long, stiff tail** often cocked upward. MALE: In breeding plumage (spring–summer) reddish-brown with black head, neck, **white cheek, powder-blue bill**; dull-brown in fall–winter (retains black cap, white cheek). FEMALE: Brownish, **light cheek crossed by dark line**.

Similar Species: Fairly unique. Female Bufflehead (page 57) has smaller bill, cheek patch.

Seasonal Abundance: Locally common winter resident in Region, uncommon breeder. Nests western North America; winters in southern U.S, along both coasts, south through Mexico. Also resident western South America.

Where to Find: Lowlands.

Habitat: Ponds, lakes, sewage lagoons; breeds at marsh-edged ponds, sloughs.

Diet and Behavior: Dives, feeds mostly on aquatic plants, some insects. Sits low in water when active but sleeps buoyantly on surface. Often in large groups when not nesting. Patters along water, flapping short wings rapidly to take flight; clumsy on land. Male courtship unique — raises tail to expose white, pumps head rapidly, followed by boisterous rushes across water.

Voice: Courting male produces stuttering series of ticks while pumping bill against inflated throat; female gives nasal call in defense of young.

Did you know? Unlike other ducks, Ruddies molt to dull plumage in fall and winter.

Date and Location Seen: _____

Male

Female

Description: 21" (male 30" with tail), wingspan 31". Large, **chicken-like** bird with **long tail**. Mostly mottled shades of brown. MALE: More colorful — orangish flanks, gray rump, **white neck-ring, iridescent-green head, red skin on face**.

Similar Species: Wild Turkey (not shown; introduced from eastern North America, occurs locally in Region) much larger, darker. Other large "chickens" in Region shorter-tailed, males drab; usually found in forests. Ruffed Grouse (page 69) smaller; Blue Grouse (page 375) gray.

Seasonal Abundance: Uncommon year-round resident in Region. Native to Asia, widely introduced as game bird elsewhere.

Where to Find: Widespread in rural, semi-rural lowlands.

Habitat: Open fields, brush patches, woodland edges, lightly developed residential areas, large parks.

Diet and Behavior: Forages on ground, also in brush, trees. Opportunistic. Consumes agricultural grains, weed seeds, roots, fruits, nuts, leaves, insects (adults, larvae), earthworms, snails. Prefers to walk or run but strong flyer when flushed. Takes off explosively on whirring wings. Young follow female, forage for themselves upon hatching. May form flocks in winter.

Voice: Male crowing, alarm call loud, grating *krrok ook*; also softer clucking sounds (both sexes).

Did you know? The first successful introduction of pheasants to the United States was in the Willamette Valley in 1882, followed by Washington in 1883.

Date and Location Seen: _____

Description: 18″, wingspan 22″. Variably brownish, cryptically patterned, **chicken-like** bird with barred flanks, **small crest** (sometimes flattened). Reddish to grayish **tail with black band near tip**.

Similar Species: Ring-necked Pheasant (page 67) much larger, long-tailed; usually found in open country. Blue Grouse (page 375) somewhat larger, tail dark with gray tip, male uniformly darker; inhabits conifer forests.

Seasonal Abundance: Fairly common year-round resident in Region. Ranges across continent's northern forest zones.

Where to Find: Widespread in foothills, Cascades, Coast Range, but secretive; usually detected by male's drumming or when female wanders into view with brood. Moves downslope in winter.

Habitat: Low- to mid-elevation deciduous or mixed forests with developed understory, ground layer, often along stream corridors.

Diet and Behavior: Leaves, fruits, other plant materials; buds important in winter. Chicks feed themselves upon hatching, mostly small invertebrates at first — can fly within week. Solitary in breeding season, may form small, loose winter flocks. Males "drum" from log, other ground perches, mostly in spring.

Voice: Unremarkable. Female sometimes makes clucking, cooing sounds.

Did you know? Drumming is an accelerating series of sonic booms as air rushes to fill the vacuum produced by the male's wing movements. Young birds require long practice to master the technique.

Date and Location Seen: _____

Male

Female

Description: 10″, wingspan 14″. Elegantly plumaged little gamefowl with **forward-drooping topknot. Grayish overall, scaled belly**, brown sides with lighter barring. MALE: Chestnut patch on belly, **white eyebrow, black throat outlined in white**. FEMALE: Head plainer, topknot smaller, no belly patch.

Similar Species: Mountain Quail (page 375) has long, straight head plume, plain belly, chestnut throat.

Seasonal Abundance: Fairly common resident in Region. Somewhat cyclical; high brood mortality in wet years. Native along Pacific Coast from southern Oregon through Baja California; introduced north to Washington, southern British Columbia.

Where to Find: Widespread in lowlands, foothills.

Habitat: Hedgerows, farm fields, clearcuts. Needs shrub cover next to open ground to forage.

Diet and Behavior: Eats mostly plant material (seeds, leaves, etc.), some invertebrates. Sociable. Coveys disband for breeding but stay within winter territory. Prolific — two broods some years, up to 20 eggs per clutch.

Voice: Loud *chi ca go* assembly call; variety of other contact, alarm, advertising calls.

Did you know? Coveys post sentries to warn of danger. Look for them on fenceposts or other prominent perches.

Date and Location Seen: _____

Non-breeding

Breeding

Description: 32″, wingspan 46″. **Large** diving bird with **thick bill**, steep forehead. NON-BREEDING: White throat, **pale around eye**; back dark with lighter mottling. **Traces of white collar extending back on upper neck, dark collar extending forward on lower neck**. BREEDING: **Head, bill black**; black collar, dark **back checkered white**.

Similar Species: Red-throated Loon (not shown; rare winter visitor on Columbia River) more finely built; thin bill held slightly upward. Pacific Loon (not shown; rare winter visitor on Columbia River, mid-elevation lakes) smaller; in winter, sharp contrast between white throat, dark back of neck.

Seasonal Abundance: Uncommon winter resident in Region; rare in summer, may nest occasionally. Breeds across northern North America to Iceland, winters south along coasts.

Where to Find: Most often seen along Columbia River, Timothy Lake, other Cascade Mountain reservoirs, but may occur on any large body of water.

Habitat: Extensive open water.

Diet and Behavior: Small fish caught, swallowed underwater. Usually forages singly.

Voice: Distinctive loud yodeling, mostly during breeding season but also sometimes in flight during migration.

Did you know? Nesting Common Loons require pristine conditions and are sensitive to human disturbance.

Date and Location Seen: _____

Breeding

Non-breeding

Description: 13", wingspan 16". **Brownish, short-necked, stocky** grebe with **thick, short, pale bill, white undertail.** BREEDING: Forehead, throat black, bill with black ring. Chicks show extensive head striping.

Similar Species: Horned Grebe (page 77) has longer, thinner bill; head, neck contrasting black-and-white in non-breeding plumage.

Seasonal Abundance: Fairly common breeder in Region, becomes common in winter as northern birds arrive. Ranges from Great Plains south to Central, South America, vacating cold interior in winter.

Where to Find: Throughout lowlands, including city parks — e.g., Crystal Springs Lake (Portland), Fern Ridge Reservoir, Fernhill Wetlands (Forest Grove). Also on higher-elevation lakes in migration.

Habitat: Marshes, vegetation-edged lakes, ponds.

Diet and Behavior: Small fish, aquatic insects, crustaceans taken underwater. To submerge, may dive headfirst or simply allow itself to sink; often resurfaces some distance away. Rarely seen in flocks.

Voice: In breeding season, loud *cuck cuck cuck, cow cow cow, cowah cowah.*

Did you know? Pied-billed Grebe is the most widespread grebe in North America and in the Region.

Date and Location Seen: _____

Eared Grebe
Non-breeding

Non-breeding

Breeding

Description: 14", wingspan 18". Relatively flat head, red eye, straight bill with light tip. Rides low in water. NON-BREEDING: Back, back of neck, crown dark-gray; **front of neck, throat, cheeks whitish**. BREEDING: Back grayish, **neck chestnut, head black with golden "ears"** from eye to back of head.

Similar Species: Eared Grebe (see inset; uncommon in Region in migration, winter) slighter, **bill thinner**; thin-necked, rides high in water. In non-breeding plumage, **cheek dark, top of head peaks above eye**. Pied-billed Grebe (page 75) overall brownish with thick bill. Western Grebe (page 79) larger with longer neck, bill.

Seasonal Abundance: Uncommon winter resident in Region (September–April). Breeds on interior lakes, marshes of northern North America, Eurasia; winters southward along coasts.

Where to Find: Widespread in lowlands; migrants to mid-elevation Cascade lakes, reservoirs.

Habitat: Sewage ponds, lakes, slow-moving rivers.

Diet and Behavior: In winter, feeds mostly on small fish obtained by diving.

Voice: Mostly silent in winter; high, thin notes occasionally heard.

Did you know? Horned Grebes can stay submerged up to three minutes and swim 500 feet below the surface on one dive.

Date and Location Seen: _____

Clark's Grebe

Description: 25", wingspan 24". **Long-necked, black-and-white** grebe with **long, thin dull-yellow bill**. Neck white in front, black behind. White throat, cheeks; black cap extends down to include red eye.

Similar Species: Clark's Grebe (see inset; uncommon, local summer resident in Region, rare in winter) almost identical but lighter-appearing; **bill orange-yellow, dark cap may not cover eye**. Red-necked Grebe (not shown; rare migrant, winter visitor in Region) has shorter neck, dark eye; in non-breeding plumage, neck gray (not white). Horned Grebe (page 77) smaller with short neck, smaller, dark bill.

Seasonal Abundance: Uncommon winter resident in Region (September–April), very local summer resident. Breeds on lakes in interior western North America; winters along coast from southeastern Alaska to northwestern Mexico.

Where to Find: Winter flocks on Columbia River, large lakes, reservoirs. Nests colonially at Fern Ridge Reservoir. Clark's Grebes usually found in close association with Westerns.

Habitat: Large lakes, rivers. Nests in vegetation at edge of open water.

Diet and Behavior: Mostly fish, obtained by diving.

Voice: Loud, high, two-note *crick creek* call, given all year.

Did you know? Western Grebes exhibit a remarkable courtship ritual, rushing along the water with extended necks and "dancing" breast to breast with weeds held in their bills.

Date and Location Seen: _____

Non-breeding

Immature

Description: 32", wingspan 52". **All-dark** with long tail, thick neck, **orange facial skin, throat pouch**. In flight, **holds thick neck with pronounced crook**. BREEDING: **White tufts behind eye**. IMMATURE: Brown with paler breast, neck.

Similar Species: Only cormorant in Region. May be mistaken for goose in flight, but longer tail, faster, intermittent wing-beats different.

Seasonal Abundance: Common winter resident in Region. A few summer, nesting at Fern Ridge Reservoir, Columbia River. Breeds on both coasts of North America, also interior of continent. Winters along coasts south to Gulf of California, Gulf of Mexico.

Where to Find: Large rivers, lakes, reservoirs. Check Willamette River in Portland, mid-elevation lakes in Cascades.

Habitat: Lakes, ponds, rivers, marshes.

Diet and Behavior: Dives for small fish. Sometimes flies high in V formation like geese. Swims low in water with head tilted slightly upward. Often perches with wings outstretched to dry. Nests colonially, mostly in shoreline trees.

Voice: Quiet away from breeding grounds.

Did you know? Double-crested Cormorant is the most widespread cormorant in North America. Rapid population increases have forced controversial control measures in some areas, to reduce predation on fish.

Date and Location Seen: _____

Description: 28", wingspan 42". Large, stocky, long-billed heron, flies with neck pulled in. **Streaked brownish**, black stripe on side of neck, **greenish legs**. Dark, pointed flight feathers contrast with back.

Similar Species: Juvenile Black-crowned Night-Heron (not shown; rare in Region) similar with rounder, even-colored wings. Juvenile Green Heron (page 89) much smaller.

Seasonal Abundance: Uncommon migrant, summer resident in Region; numbers fall in winter. Ranges across North America, winters to Central America.

Where to Find: Lowland marshes. Best spot Killin Wetlands (Banks).

Habitat: Large, open marshes with some tall, dense vegetation.

Diet and Behavior: Secretive, usually solitary. Forages stealthily, mostly at water, for fish and other animal life (insects, crustaceans, frogs, small mammals). Hides motionless with neck extended, bill pointing up, protective coloration blending in with vegetation. Nests on ground in marsh, rarely perches in trees like other herons.

Voice: Sometimes called "thunder-pumper" for deep, pump-like *boonk ahh* song produced by gulping, then expelling air from swollen esophagus. Also squawks in alarm.

Did you know? American Bittern populations are shrinking across their range due to the disappearance of large, undisturbed wetland habitats.

Date and Location Seen: _____

Description: 48″, wingspan 72″. **Long-necked**, long-legged wader with formidable **dagger-like bill**. Mostly bluish-gray above, lighter below, **white face topped with black crest**. In flight neck usually pulled in, legs trail behind; wings broad, slightly cupped. JUVENILE, NON-BREEDING: Duller.

Similar Species: Great Egret (page 87) slightly smaller, all-white. Black-crowned Night-Heron (not shown; rare in Region) somewhat similar in plumage but considerably smaller with short neck, bill.

Seasonal Abundance: Common resident in Region. Ranges across North America from southern Alaska to Maritimes, south to northern South America.

Where to Find: Throughout Region.

Habitat: Marshes, ponds, agricultural fields, rivers, lakes.

Diet and Behavior: Forages by standing or walking slowly, equally likely in water or fields. Extremely varied diet includes any animal life that can be grasped or speared with bill; rodents important component in Region. Nests primarily in colonies in tall dead or dying trees.

Voice: Loud croaking, often drawn-out *frahhhnnk*, usually given when flushed.

Did you know? Great Blue Herons may be mistaken for Sandhill Cranes (page 123) but are not related to the cranes, which never fly with their necks pulled in as herons do.

Date and Location Seen: _____

Description: 39", wingspan 44". Wading bird with **long black legs, black feet**, long neck, long yellow bill, **all-white plumage**. Usually flies with neck pulled in.

Similar Species: Great Blue Heron (page 85) sturdier, mostly blue-gray. Two other white egrets half the size (neither shown; both rare in Region). Snowy Egret with dark bill, yellow feet. Cattle Egret with yellowish legs, much shorter neck, bill.

Seasonal Abundance: Fairly common to locally common, increasing winter resident in Region; uncommon summer, occasionally nests. Ranges worldwide across temperate zones, tropics; in U.S., northern, interior breeding populations move south or to coasts in winter.

Where to Find: Throughout lowlands. Best bets Fern Ridge Reservoir, Sauvie Island, Ridgefield National Wildlife Refuge.

Habitat: Lakes, sloughs, agricultural fields, wetlands. Nests, roosts in trees, usually colonially, often with Great Blue Herons.

Diet and Behavior: Hunts by slow stalking or by stand-and-wait strategy, striking with bill to impale or seize large insects, crustaceans, small fish, frogs, lizards, snakes, small mammals.

Voice: Mostly silent outside nesting season. Squawks, croaks as alarm or warning, greeting at roosts.

Did you know? Plume-hunting for women's hats brought Great Egrets nearly to the brink of extinction. Populations rebounded after conservationists won protection for the species through passage of the Migratory Bird Treaty Act (1913).

Date and Location Seen: _____

Juvenile

Description: 17", wingspan 26". **Crow-sized**, relatively short-necked heron; flies with legs trailing, neck pulled in. ADULT: Dark-greenish above, purplish-rufous below, white streaking at breast center, **orangish legs**. JUVENILE: Upperparts brown, underparts white with brown streaking, legs duller.

Similar Species: Juvenile Black-crowned Night-Heron (not shown; rare in Region) larger, with heavier bill. American Bittern (page 83) streaked beneath like juvenile Green Heron, but much larger.

Seasonal Abundance: Uncommon summer resident in Region, rare in winter. Ranges across U.S. to southern Canada, rare in western interior; winters to Central America. Populations slowly increasing in western Oregon, farther north along Pacific Coast.

Where to Find: Lowland lakes, rivers. Check Crystal Springs Lake (Portland), Fern Ridge Reservoir (Eugene).

Habitat: Sheltered ponds, streams, with wooded edges.

Diet and Behavior: Secretive, usually solitary. Forages both day, night, mostly at water, primarily for fish but also other animal life. Very agile, sometimes hanging upside down to capture prey. Nests in trees, sometimes near neighborhoods.

Voice: Loud *kyow*.

Did you know? Green Herons are known to use bait, such as a feather or twig dropped on the water, to lure inquisitive fish to the surface.

Date and Location Seen: _____

Description: 26", wingspan 66". Blackish, long-tailed, with small, bare **red head**; soars on long, fairly broad, two-toned **wings held above horizontal in tipping, unsteady flight**. Appears plump when perched. JUVENILE: Black head.

Similar Species: Immature Bald Eagle (page 97), Red-tailed Hawk (page 107) soar with wings held flatter; heads larger, different underwing patterns. Northern Harrier (page 99) similar in flight but rump white.

Seasonal Abundance: Fairly common summer resident in Region, mid-February to October. Ranges from southern Canada to South America.

Where to Find: Throughout Region up to mountain passes, scarce near cities.

Habitat: Open areas such as agricultural fields, clearcuts, in proximity to forested hills.

Diet and Behavior: Soars, searching for dead animals by sight, smell. Seldom flaps, relying on thermals for soaring. Gregarious, usually roosting, migrating, feeding in groups. Reluctantly crosses water bodies in migration, waiting for favorable winds — resulting at times in concentrated migratory flights.

Voice: Grunting, hissing (seldom heard).

Did you know? Turkey Vultures were long considered to be a type of raptor, like hawks and eagles. However, recent studies have proved them to be closely related to the storks.

Date and Location Seen: _____

OSPREY
Pandion haliaetus

Description: 23″, wingspan 63″. **Blackish above** except for **whitish crown**. Mostly **white underparts** contrast with **dark mask**, strongly banded wings, tail. Wings long, somewhat angled (gull-like) with dark patch at wrist.

Similar Species: Immature Bald Eagle (page 97) may appear similar with white belly, dark mask on white head, but upper breast dark. Gulls have more-pointed wings.

Seasonal Abundance: Fairly common, increasing summer resident in Region, arrives late March, most depart by October but a few linger — very rarely to winter. Range worldwide; northern birds winter to southern continents.

Where to Find: Throughout Region; good concentrations at Fern Ridge Reservoir, Sauvie Island.

Habitat: Usually near water, but migrants may be anywhere.

Diet and Behavior: Feeds almost exclusively on live fish, hovering over water, plunging feet-first, sometimes catching prey well below surface. Feet equipped with bumps called spicules that assist talons in holding fish. Pairs raise young on top of broken tree, power tower, platform, building bulky nest, often near human habitation. May be loosely colonial.

Voice: Noisy, calling with slurred, shrill whistles.

Did you know? Osprey populations are rebounding rapidly from a DDT-caused population decline. Power companies take measures to protect birds nesting on utility poles from electrocution and to lessen the danger of power outages.

Date and Location Seen: _____

Description: 15″, wingspan 40″. **Graceful** falcon-shaped raptor, light-gray above with **black shoulder patches**. Head, **long tail, underparts white**, eye red, long wings dark at tips, black wrist patch below. Often **hovers**, flies with wings held above horizontal. IMMATURE: Browner above, light-rufous streaks below.

Similar Species: Male Northern Harrier (page 99) has gray tail, white rump. Gulls, terns differently shaped, lack shoulder patches.

Seasonal Abundance: Uncommon resident, rare breeder, numbers augmented from August through March by post-breeding birds dispersing from farther south. Range southern Washington down coast to Mexico, South America; also Texas, Florida.

Where to Find: Sparsely in open areas throughout lowlands. Good spots include Fern Ridge Reservoir, Finley National Wildlife Refuge, locations near Columbia River.

Habitat: Grasslands, meadows; uncultivated farmland with scattered trees, shrubby edge; marsh along river valleys.

Diet and Behavior: Hunts rodents, rarely insects, small birds from extended stationary hovering. Perches prominently in open. Gregarious in fall, winter — may roost in large groups. Secretive in nesting season; nests in tops of small trees.

Voice: Whistles, chirps, grating calls, seldom heard.

Did you know? Once considered endangered, White-tailed Kites have expanded their range from California into Oregon and southern Washington during the last 60 years.

Date and Location Seen: _____

First-year

First-year

Description: 33″, wingspan 82″. ADULT: Dark-brown with **white head, tail**; huge yellow bill, feet, eye. Soars on **long, broad wings**. FIRST-YEAR: Lacks white head, tail; bill, eye dark. Birds transition to adult plumage, bill, eye color over four years.

Similar Species: Hawks have shorter wings. Golden Eagle (not shown; uncommon in Region) has golden feathers on nape, smaller head, bill; immature with white patches at center of wing, base of tail.

Seasonal Abundance: Common resident in Region, harder to find in early fall when disperses to north. Ranges Alaska to Labrador, south to northern Mexico.

Where to Find: Widespread, mostly along rivers, lakes; best bet Sauvie Island.

Habitat: Farmlands, lakes, rivers, ponds; nest usually near water.

Diet and Behavior: Feeds mostly on fish when available, including spawned-out salmon in rivers, also water birds, geese, carrion, other prey; steals food from smaller raptors. Pairs return to territories in mid-fall, may work on nests; eggs laid by early March, young fledge by late July.

Voice: Far-carrying call — series of chirping whistles, piercing screams.

Did you know? After breeding, many Bald Eagles leave the Willamette Valley Region to track migrating salmon, moving to northern rivers for the earlier spawning runs and southern rivers for the late-fall/winter runs.

Date and Location Seen: _____

Female

Male

NORTHERN HARRIER
Circus cyaneus

Description: 19", wingspan 44". Slim, **long-winged**, with **owl-like face**, long, banded tail, **white rump**. Usually flies with **wings held above horizontal**. MALE: Adult gray (whiter below) with black wingtips. FEMALE: Larger; brown above, streaked below. IMMATURE: Resembles female, but juvenile orangish on breast, lacking streaks.

Similar Species: White rump distinctive. Rough-legged Hawk (page 109) has white tail base, not rump. Red-tailed Hawk (page 107) has broader wings. Cooper's Hawk (page 103) smaller, holds wings flatter. Falcons have more-pointed wings, swifter flight.

Seasonal Abundance: Locally common migrant, winter resident in Region, uncommon breeder. Ranges across northern hemisphere, winters to northern tropics. North American population sometimes considered separate species.

Where to Find: Lowlands; migrants rarely in mountains, urban areas.

Habitat: Open terrain including marshes, fields, agricultural flats, sometimes clearcuts.

Diet and Behavior: Courses low, "harries" prey, using vision, hearing to locate movement, then dives to flush, catch small mammals, birds. May hover briefly. Concentrates at productive locations to hunt, roost. Nests on ground.

Voice: Calls include whistles, also rapid chatter heard while breeding, occasionally on winter quarters.

Did you know? Male Northern Harriers may mate with several females. Courting pairs perform spectacular roller-coaster flights and prey transfers high in the air.

Date and Location Seen: _____

Immature

Description: 12", wingspan 24" (averages; female larger than male). **Small**, slim, short-winged hawk with **long, matchstick-thin yellow legs**, broadly banded, **long, square-tipped tail**. Alternates rapid flapping with gliding. ADULT: Barred reddish-brown below, head, back gray, eye bright-red. IMMATURE: Brownish back, heavily streaked brown-and-white below, eye yellow.

Similar Species: Cooper's Hawk (page 103) nearly identical, but larger, tail rounder at tip; adult has "capped", sometimes square-headed appearance. Size separation tricky — female Sharp-shinned barely smaller than male Cooper's. American Kestrel (page 111), Merlin (page 113) have pointed wings.

Seasonal Abundance: Fairly common migrant in Region, less common in winter; uncommon breeder. Ranges from Alaska to Labrador, winters south to Central America.

Where to Find: Throughout Region.

Habitat: Breeds in dense conifer or mixed forest. Migrants, winter birds in broken woodland, brushy areas, neighborhoods.

Diet and Behavior: Feeds almost exclusively on birds, often near bird feeders. Bursts forth from hidden perch to surprise prey in low, rapid flight. Often shadows migrating songbird flocks. Pugnacious if concealed nest discovered.

Voice: Series of high-pitched *kews*.

Did you know? Many Sharp-shinned Hawks remain year round in their breeding range, but disperse widely in fall using thermals to assist travel and to locate prey while soaring.

Date and Location Seen: _____

Immature

Description: 17", wingspan 33" (averages; female larger than male). **Lanky**, short-winged hawk, **long, yellow, pencil-sized legs, long, broadly banded tail**. Soars with wings held straight across. ADULT: Barred reddish-brown below, **dark-gray cap**, grayish back, pale-gray neck, eye reddish. IMMATURE: Brown back, white with brown streaks below, eye yellow.

Similar Species: Sharp-shinned Hawk (page 101) almost identical but smaller, with thinner legs, tail squarer at tip. Adult lacks "capped" appearance, soars with wrists held forward. Size separation tricky — male Cooper's only slightly larger than female Sharp-shinned. Red-shouldered Hawk (page 105) bulkier, with narrower bands on shorter tail. Northern Goshawk (page 377) adult gray, juvenile heavily streaked to undertail.

Seasonal Abundance: Fairly common migrant, resident in Region. Secretive nester, much more evident in other seasons. Ranges across continent, southern Canada to Central America.

Where to Find: Throughout Region.

Habitat: Forest, broken woodland, farms, neighborhoods.

Diet and Behavior: Ambushes prey from hidden perch with rapid burst of speed, also cruises, searches; often stakes out bird feeders. Takes mostly birds, also small mammals while nesting. Disperses widely in fall although many remain year round in breeding range.

Voice: Calls include repeated *kek*, nasal squawks.

Did you know? Cooper's Hawks sometimes breed at one year, while still in juvenal plumage.

Date and Location Seen: _____

Immature

Description: 17", wingspan 40". Relatively long-tailed, soaring hawk. **Tail black with 4–5 white bands, wings checkered black-and-white**, shoulder rusty. Light, transverse, translucent crescents near wingtip visible in flight. ADULT: Reddish barring below, underwing rusty. IMMATURE: Variable, browner, **evenly streaked, mottled below**, tail bands narrower.

Similar Species: Immature Red-tailed Hawk (page 107) has larger head, bill; clear, white upper breast contrasting with dark belly band; numerous fine tail bands. Cooper's Hawk (page 103) lanky, tail longer with wider bands.

Seasonal Abundance: Fairly common winter resident in Region (August–March); locally uncommon in summer, breeds sparsely. Two disjunct populations: West Coast (Washington to Baja California), eastern United States.

Where to Find: Throughout lowlands, e.g., Killin Wetlands (Banks), Ridgefield National Wildlife Refuge, Fern Ridge Reservoir. More common in southern part of Region.

Habitat: Moist deciduous woodlands, stream bottoms, in proximity to wet meadows.

Diet and Behavior: Snakes, amphibians, small birds, mammals, captured mostly by flying from perch. Tends to remain hidden in tree canopy, but fairly vocal, so often detected by voice.

Voice: High-pitched, repeated, two-note *kee yar*.

Did you know? Range expansion brought the Red-shouldered Hawk to the Willamette Valley from California during the 1970s.

Date and Location Seen: _____

Immature

Description: 20", wingspan 48". Bulky. Soars on **broad wings** held flat. **Dark line on leading edge of underwing** from neck to wrist, **dark head**, streaked band across belly. ADULT: Reddish tail. IMMATURE: Brown, finely banded tail, whiter breast. DARK MORPH: Adult brown, except lighter flight feathers. HARLAN'S: Usually blackish, lacks brown tones; tail whitish.

Similar Species: Rough-legged Hawk (page 109) has white tail with black tip, whitish head, dark wrist marks on underwings, soars with wings held above horizontal. Eagles (page 97) have longer wings.

Seasonal Abundance: Common resident in Region, numbers augmented by migrants, wintering birds. Dark morph uncommon; Harlan's uncommon winter visitor. Ranges across North America south of tree line, to Central America.

Where to Find: Nearly anywhere.

Habitat: Open habitats, edges — highly adaptable. Fields, freeway corridors, clearcuts, open woods.

Diet and Behavior: Hunts for wide variety of prey, mostly from perch, swooping to capture prey in talons. Also soars, sometimes "kites" in stationary hover in wind. Will take carrion. Protects territory year round, calling at intruders.

Voice: Most common call rasping, down-slurred scream.

Did you know? Red-tailed Hawks come in an amazing assortment of plumages. Variation among regional populations, color morphs, ages, and even individuals can make this common species difficult to identify.

Date and Location Seen: _____

Light Morph

Immature Light Morph

Dark Morph

Description: 21″, wingspan 53″. Broad-winged, bulky, soaring hawk with **highly variable** plumage dependent on sex, age, color morph. Key marks include **white tail with wide black tip, whitish head** with dark eye-line, small bill, **white upper breast**, dark belly, white underwings with **dark wrist patches**. Less common dark morph appears blackish except for white flight feathers contrasting with front of underwing.

Similar Species: Red-tailed Hawk (page 107) immature may appear similar, especially when hovering, but wings less pointed, held flatter; underwing lacks wrist mark, instead has dark line on leading edge.

Seasonal Abundance: Uncommon, local winter resident in Region, arrives October, departs by April. Breeds on Arctic tundra in North America, Eurasia, winters to temperate latitudes.

Where to Find: Lowlands; widespread in migration. Baskett Slough, Ridgefield National Wildlife Refuges good bets.

Habitat: Open areas: agricultural fields, prairies, marshes.

Diet and Behavior: Hunts mostly for small mammals from perch or by hovering in place; also takes birds, carrion. Soars with wings held above horizontal. Often perches on twigs that appear small for its bulk. Sometimes forms communal roosts in winter.

Voice: Seldom heard except when nesting.

Did you know? Rough-legged Hawks often return to the same winter range — year after year, if it continues to produce their preferred rodent prey.

Date and Location Seen: _____

Male

Female

Description: 10″, wingspan 21″. **Delicate**, long-tailed falcon with **long, pointed wings, russet back**, gray-and-rufous crown, **two black stripes on white face**. MALE: Wings blue-gray above, solid russet tail ending in wide black band, narrow white tip. Breast rusty in adult, streaked in immature. FEMALE: Similar; wings, tail russet with fine banding, breast streaked.

Similar Species: Merlin (page 113) chunkier; darkly streaked below with broadly banded tail, vague mustache mark, more powerful flight.

Seasonal Abundance: Fairly common resident in Region. Ranges across North America south of tree line, winters as far south as Central America.

Where to Find: Widespread, conspicuous, mainly in lowlands.

Habitat: Open areas such as farmland, alpine meadows, forest edges, clearings.

Diet and Behavior: Hunts for insects, small mammals, small birds from perches or by stationary hovering over field. Nests in natural cavities (usually trees) but also uses nest boxes. Defends territory by calling, flying at intruders.

Voice: Common call series of piercing *kli* notes.

Did you know? American Kestrels are migratory over much of their range, but most Willamette Valley birds remain year round.

Date and Location Seen: _____

Description: 11", wingspan 23". Compact, **swift-flying**, small falcon. Plumage varies with race, but generally **heavily streaked below** with plain, dark back, **banded tail, vague mustache mark**. Appears dark in flight with **sharply pointed wings**. MALE: Adult with gray back, cap. FEMALE: Larger, browner. JUVENILE: Brown.

Similar Species: Peregrine Falcon (page 115) larger with prominent mustache mark. American Kestrel (page 111) lighter below, finely built, with distinct head markings.

Seasonal Abundance: Fairly common but easily overlooked migrant, winter resident in Region. Ranges across northern forests of Eurasia, North America, winters to southern tropics.

Where to Find: Mostly lowlands. Easiest to find in cities, towns, or near concentrations of Dunlins.

Habitat: Marshes, agricultural flats, broken woodlands, urban areas.

Diet and Behavior: Makes dashing flights from perch, captures prey with talons at blinding speed. Diet almost exclusively small songbirds, shorebirds. Rarely soars; typical flight observation bullet-like pass. More likely spotted perched atop prominent snags, conifers. Aggressively harasses other raptors many times its size.

Voice: Rarely vocal away from nest; calls include series of *twi* notes.

Did you know? Falcons do not exhibit nest-building behavior. Instead they use old nests of other birds, ledges, or cavities. Merlins most often use old crow nests.

Date and Location Seen: _____

Immature

Description: 16″, wingspan 43″. Sleek, powerfully built, **crow-sized** falcon with **thick mustache mark**, long **wings reaching tail tip when perched**. Gray above, dark barring below, variable salmon-colored or whitish bib. **Sharply pointed wings** in flight. IMMATURE: Browner with streaking instead of barring; bill, skin around eye pale-blue (yellow in adult).

Similar Species: Merlin (page 113) smaller, mustache mark less distinct. Two other falcons (neither shown; both rare in Region). Prairie Falcon browner with dark armpits; Gyrfalcon bulkier with shorter, broader wings.

Seasonal Abundance: Uncommon resident in Region, numbers augmented by migrants, wintering birds late September–May. Many races range worldwide.

Where to Find: Most common in lowlands. Often found near waterfowl, shorebird concentrations; best bets include mid-town Portland.

Habitat: Open areas, rivers, lakes, wetlands; nests on buildings, bridges, cliffs, other tall structures.

Diet and Behavior: Catches live birds in mid-air, making spectacular dives at speeds up to 200 miles per hour. Prey ranges from songbirds to ducks; Rock Pigeons, shorebirds favored. Rarely eats mammals, carrion. Nests on bare ledge, fiercely defends territory.

Voice: Calls include harsh, piercing series of *keh* notes.

Did you know? Peregrine Falcons were taken off the Endangered Species List in 1999 after numbers rebounded from pesticide-caused declines.

Date and Location Seen: _____

Description: 10″. Long-legged marsh bird with **reddish-brown breast**, gray face, **long, thin, slightly downcurved red bill**, banded black-and-white flanks, short tail (often cocked upward). JUVENILE: Smaller, duskier.

Similar Species: Sora (page 119) similar in size, behavior, habitat preferences, but has gray breast, shorter, thicker yellow bill, black face.

Seasonal Abundance: Fairly common resident in Region, nesting at low to middle elevations, moving to lowlands in winter. Breeds across North America from southern Canada south, except for lower Great Plains, Southeast; winters along coasts, in Mexico. Also resident in South America.

Where to Find: Anywhere with suitable habitat, e.g., Killin Wetlands (Banks), Fern Ridge Reservoir.

Habitat: Pond edges, marshes, roadside ditches. Needs shallow standing water, emergent vegetation.

Diet and Behavior: Largely animal diet — insects, larvae, snails, spiders, small frogs, small fish; some vegetal material. Probes with bill in mud, shallow water, dead vegetation. Weak flier; mostly runs or walks, staying well-hidden.

Voice: Calls include *kiddik kiddik kiddik* in breeding season; series of grunts, often in duet, throughout year.

Did you know? Virginia Rails have flexible vertebrae to help them thread their way through dense standing vegetation, and long toes for walking on floating mats.

Date and Location Seen: _____

Description: 9″. Brownish-black rail with **stubby yellow bill**; long greenish legs, toes; barred flanks. ADULT: **Throat, front of face black; breast gray**. JUVENILE: Lacks black on face, throat; breast buffy; bill, legs duller.

Similar Species: Virginia Rail (page 117) similar in size, behavior, habitat preferences, but with long red bill, reddish-brown breast.

Seasonal Abundance: Common migrant, summer resident in Region; uncommon in winter. Breeds from southeastern Alaska to Maritimes, south to Middle Atlantic, northern Plains states, intermountain West. Winters along U.S. coasts, throughout Middle America, West Indies, to northern South America.

Where to Find: Lowland wetlands, e.g., Killin Wetlands (Banks), Ridgefield National Wildlife Refuge, Fern Ridge Reservoir.

Habitat: Thick vegetated shorelines, shallow marshes; prefers extensive tracts for nesting but also uses small, seasonal wetlands, wet fields, especially in migration.

Diet and Behavior: Seeds of sedges, other wetland plants; also leaves, stems, other plant material. Secondarily insects, other invertebrates. Remains well-hidden in vegetation. Excellent swimmer, often observed crossing open water.

Voice: Loud, distinctive calls given day or night, mostly in breeding season: clear, rising *kah weee*, falling whinny. Also sharp *keek*.

Did you know? The Sora is primarily vegetarian whereas the Virginia Rail has a largely animal diet, enabling these two closely related species to share the same habitat.

Date and Location Seen: _____

Description: 15″, wingspan 26″. **Dark-gray** aquatic bird, undertail edged in white. **Black head, red iris, pointed white bill with band near tip, white forehead shield** (dark-red or brown at top). Legs greenish to yellowish, **long lobed toes**. JUVENILE: Paler, legs gray, no red on forehead shield.

Similar Species: Distinctive. Pied-billed Grebe (page 75) brown.

Seasonal Abundance: Fairly common summer resident in Region, common winter resident. Nests western half of North America, Midwest; winters along coasts, in southern U.S., south to Costa Rica.

Where to Find: Widespread. In winter often forms large rafts on low-to-mid-elevation lakes, reservoirs, sewage ponds.

Habitat: Breeds in shallow freshwater lakes, wetlands, with emergent vegetation, open water. Winters on lakes, ponds.

Diet and Behavior: Dives or tips up in shallow water, grazes on lawns, fields. Eats mostly plants, a few invertebrates. Needs long takeoff path, splashing strides on water, until airborne.

Voice: *Puck* notes singly or in series; array of other cackling, clucking, crowing calls.

Did you know? Wigeons and Gadwalls often swim with American Coots, wait for them to surface, and steal the aquatic vegetation they bring up.

Date and Location Seen: _____

Description: 44", wingspan 76". Long legs, neck. Mostly **light-gray with prominent "bustle"**; outer flight feathers black. ADULT: **Red crown, white cheeks**; body feathers often stained brown in summer. JUVENILE: Lacks red crown; head, neck pale-chestnut; gray body feathers edged rusty-brown.

Similar Species: Herons, egrets in Region (pages 85–89) nest, roost in trees; usually fly with neck pulled in. Cranes fly with neck extended; nest on ground, do not perch.

Seasonal Abundance: Locally common migrant, winter resident in Region; nests sparingly in wet meadows in Cascades. Breeds northeast Siberia to Hudson's Bay, south to Michigan, locally Colorado, California; winters southwestern U.S., Mexico. Sedentary populations in Mississippi, Florida, Cuba.

Where to Find: Large open areas. Winters primarily Sauvie Island, Ridgefield National Wildlife Refuge. Migrates in narrow pathway over central Willamette Valley.

Habitat: Wetlands, meadows, farm fields, mudflats about shallow lakes.

Diet and Behavior: Picks, probes on ground, in shallow water, for wide variety of plant, animal material. Sociable; communicates through "dancing", other body movements, vocalizations.

Voice: Adults give far-carrying (1-2 miles), bugling rattle in flight or on ground; juvenile has harsh trill.

Did you know? Sandhill Cranes form lifelong pair bonds. Parents remain with young until the next nesting season.

Date and Location Seen: _____

Breeding

Non-breeding

Description: 11". Plump, with **short bill**, relatively short, blackish legs; **black armpits** visible in flight. BREEDING: Adults show **black face, breast, belly**, whitish crown, neck, sides, undertail, spangled back. Female, molting birds browner, less distinctly marked. NON-BREEDING: Speckled brownish-gray above with indistinct whitish eyebrow, plainer below. JUVENILE: Browner with grayish legs.

Similar Species: Distinctive in breeding plumage; bill shorter than other large shorebirds. American, Pacific Golden-Plovers (neither shown; both rare in Region) slightly smaller, lack black armpit; more golden in summer, browner in fall.

Seasonal Abundance: Uncommon migrant, winter resident in Region. Breeds on Arctic tundra around northern hemisphere, winters to southern continents.

Where to Find: Lowlands. Fern Ridge Reservoir best bet.

Habitat: Mudflats, short-grass or plowed fields, open marsh.

Diet and Behavior: Forages visually by running, stopping, picking food from ground; also may probe. Diet mostly worms, insects, marine organisms. Birds spread out to feed but roost in groups, often flocking with other shorebirds, especially Dunlins.

Voice: Very vocal. Most common call forlorn-sounding, whistled *plee o weee*.

Did you know? This widespread species is known in Eurasia as the Gray Plover.

Date and Location Seen: _____

Description: 7″. Plain grayish-brown above except for **white-and-black collar, forehead**, black cheek; **white below with black breast band. Bill short** with pinkish-orange base; pinkish-yellow legs short. White wing stripe on long wings visible in flight. JUVENILE: Duller, with dark bill.

Similar Species: Shorter bill separates from sandpipers. Killdeer (page 129) larger with double breast band; juvenile Killdeer usually appears fluffy.

Seasonal Abundance: Fairly common but local migrant in Region (April–May, mid-July–October). Rare in winter. Breeds across North American Arctic, subarctic, winters as far south as South America.

Where to Find: Lowlands; Fern Ridge Reservoir good spot.

Habitat: Mudflats, lake edges, agricultural fields.

Diet and Behavior: Forages visually by running, stopping, picking food from ground. Feeds on aquatic organisms, insects. Usually in flocks, associates loosely with other shorebirds.

Voice: Common flight call whistled *chu wee*. Trills, chatters during interactions with others of its species.

Did you know? Semipalmated Plover gets its name from its partially webbed feet.

Date and Location Seen: _____

Description: 10". Plain brown above with white collar, **white below except for two black breast bands**. Forehead, eyebrow white; **bill dark, short**; legs relatively short, yellowish. **Orange tail, rump**, white wing stripe visible in flight. Scarlet eye-ring. JUVENILE: One breast band when half-grown.

Similar Species: Semipalmated Plover (page 127) smaller with one breast band, shorter bill, lacks orange rump.

Seasonal Abundance: Common resident in Region. Ranges from Alaska, Newfoundland to South America; withdraws from coldest areas in winter.

Where to Find: Mostly lowlands. Forms large post-breeding flocks on farm fields in late summer, continuing through winter.

Habitat: Open habitats without high grass — lawns, road edges, beaches, mudflats, plowed fields, parking lots. Prefers bare gravel near water for nesting.

Diet and Behavior: Forages visually by running, stopping, picking food from ground. Feeds mostly on insects, also some seeds. Secretive at open nest site but calls, feigns broken wing as part of distraction display when discovered.

Voice: Varied strident calls include *kill deeah, deee*, and *dee ahy*. Gives high, rapid trill when nervous.

Did you know? The Killdeer's four black-spotted green eggs are nearly invisible in their gravel nest when left unattended.

Date and Location Seen: _____

Greater Yellowlegs Breeding

Greater Yellowlegs Juvenile

Lesser Yellowlegs Breeding

Lesser Yellowlegs Juvenile

GREATER YELLOWLEGS / LESSER YELLOWLEGS
Tringa melanoleuca / Tringa flavipes

Description: 14" / 10 ". Elegant, grayish waders with **long, bright-yellowish-orange legs**, long neck, fairly long, mostly dark bill, whitish speckling on dark back. Lighter below, with **plain wings, white rump** visible in flight. Breast streaked in breeding plumage. GREATER: More robust, thicker legs, **bill longer, slightly upturned**, pale-based. LESSER: More **delicate; bill shorter, straighter**.

Similar Species: Solitary Sandpiper (not shown; rare in Region) slightly smaller than Lesser, with greenish legs, white eye-ring.

Seasonal Abundance: Fairly common migrants in Region. GREATER: Arrives July, a few linger in winter; returns March–April. Breeds southern Alaska to Labrador, winters to South America. LESSER: Arrives by July, departs by October, rarely winters; uncommon in spring. Breeds Alaska to central Canada, winters to South America.

Where to Find: Lowlands.

Habitat: Flooded fields, marshes, shallow ponds.

Diet and Behavior: Forage in shallow water, swinging bill side to side or running after small fish, insects, other organisms; often flock, sometimes with other shorebirds.

Voice: Call *tew*, repeated 3–4 times in GREATER, 2–3 times in LESSER; both *tew* continuously in alarm.

Did you know? A pair of Greater Yellowlegs nested four years running in Wallowa County, Oregon, 500 miles south of the species' normal breeding range.

Date and Location Seen: _____

Breeding

Non-breeding

Description: 8″. Small, with **short reddish bill**, short yellowish legs, **white wing stripe** visible in flight, white eye-line, **constant teetering motion**. BREEDING: **Dark spots** on white underparts, bill brighter red. NON-BREEDING: Evenly grayish-brown above to dusky neck; **white underparts extend up side in front of folded wing**. JUVENILE: White edges on wing feathers.

Similar Species: Solitary Sandpiper (not shown; rare in Region) also teeters; taller, with greenish legs, fine white back spotting, strong white eye-ring, lacks black eye-line.

Seasonal Abundance: Fairly common summer resident in Region; rare in winter. Ranges across North America, winters to South America.

Where to Find: Widespread, from lowlands to mountains.

Habitat: Nests at gravelly areas with sparse vegetation along streams, lakes, sewage ponds; winters about lowland rivers, ponds, lakes.

Diet and Behavior: Forages visually by picking, chasing, fluttering after insects, small organisms, tiny fish; may take carrion. Highly territorial at all seasons so does not flock. Distinctive flapping flight: short pulses with wings not raised above horizontal, alternating with glides on bowed wings.

Voice: Loud, repeated, clear, high-pitched whistles.

Did you know? Spotted Sandpiper is one of a small number of shorebird species where females sometimes mate with more than one male.

Date and Location Seen: _____

Breeding

Non-breeding

Juvenile

Description: 6¼". Small sandpiper, brownish-gray with evenly tapered, **drooping, fine-tipped bill, blackish legs**, white belly, whitish eye-line; thin white wing stripe visible in flight. BREEDING: **Rufous highlights in back, head feathers**, black chevron marks on flanks. NON-BREEDING: Evenly grayish-brown with white underparts. JUVENILE: Paler, less strongly marked version of breeding adult.

Similar Species: Semipalmated Sandpiper (not shown; rare migrant in Region) has blunt, short bill, little or no rufous coloring. Baird's Sandpiper (not shown; uncommon fall migrant in Region) slightly larger with thin, straight bill, folded wings longer than tail. Sanderling (not shown; rare migrant in Region) larger, with shorter, blunt bill. Least Sandpiper (page 137) has yellow legs.

Seasonal Abundance: Common migrant in Region, July–November; a few winter. Breeding-plumaged flocks present spring, early summer. Breeds Alaska west to Siberia, winters coastally to South America.

Where to Find: Widespread in lowlands.

Habitat: Open shoreline, mudflats, muddy fields.

Diet and Behavior: Probes, picks small organisms from mud; may eat seeds. Feeds, roosts in flocks with other shorebirds.

Voice: Flight call thin *dcheet*. Feeding flocks may chatter.

Did you know? Western Sandpiper is the most abundant migrant shorebird in Oregon. Flocks of thousands are often encountered in the Willamette Valley Region.

Date and Location Seen: _____

Breeding

Non-breeding

Juvenile

Description: 5½". **Smallest sandpiper**, brownish with **short, fine-tipped, drooping bill, yellowish legs, brownish upper breast**, white belly, white lines down back; thin white wing stripe visible in flight. BREEDING: Darker with black centers on back feathers. NON-BREEDING: Evenly grayish-brown with whitish belly. JUVENILE: More rufous than adult, legs duller.

Similar Species: Western Sandpiper (page 135), Baird's Sandpiper (not shown; uncommon fall migrant in Region) have black legs. Baird's larger with thin, straight bill. Pectoral Sandpiper (page 139) similar but much larger, legs proportionally longer.

Seasonal Abundance: Common migrant in Region (April–May, July–October), uncommon in winter. Breeds in north from Alaska to Labrador, winters south to northern South America.

Where to Find: Throughout Region, mostly in lowlands.

Habitat: Mudflats, pond margins, marshes, muddy pools, ditches.

Diet and Behavior: Forages mostly by picking, sometimes probing, primarily for insects, aquatic organisms; may eat some plant material. Frequently in small groups rather than large flocks. Not shy, often allowing close approach.

Voice: Flight call *pree eet*. Birds may utter *dee dee dee* call among themselves.

Did you know? The small North American sandpipers (including Least and Western) are often referred to collectively as "peeps", together with the stints of Eurasia.

Date and Location Seen: _____

Description: 9". **Medium-sized**, streaky, brownish sandpiper, with moderately heavy, slightly drooping bill, **yellowish legs**. Grayish-brown **upper breast abruptly contrasts with white belly**. Long, dark wings show only weak, light stripe in flight.

Similar Species: Least Sandpiper (page 137) similar, but much smaller with less distinct lower breast border. Baird's Sandpiper (not shown; uncommon fall migrant in Region) smaller with dark legs, straight bill. Sharp-tailed Sandpiper (not shown; rare fall migrant in Region) with distinct reddish cap, peachy-buff breast. Dowitchers (page 143) have much longer bills.

Seasonal Abundance: Variable year to year in Region. Uncommon to fairly common or even common fall migrant (July–November), rare to absent other seasons. Breeds on tundra from eastern Siberia to central Canada, winters to South America.

Where to Find: Widespread; mainly lowlands.

Habitat: Open flats, plowed farm fields, marshes, wet meadows, grassy spots along pond margins.

Diet and Behavior: Picks, probes, primarily for insects, aquatic organisms. Tends to forage quietly in small groups in or close to vegetation on drier parts of flats; detection difficult at times.

Voice: Low, harsh, reedy *drrrit* in flight.

Did you know? Most Pectoral Sandpipers seen in the Willamette Valley Region are juveniles. Flocks are often approachable and tame.

Date and Location Seen: _____

Breeding

Non-breeding

Description: 8½". Fairly small, **hunched appearance**, with **short, dark legs, long, dark bill with drooping tip**; white wing stripe visible in flight. BREEDING: Spring birds mostly **rufous above with black belly**, whitish face, upper breast. NON-BREEDING: **Plain brownish-gray** with white belly, underwing, faint eye-line.

Similar Species: Larger with longer bill than other small shorebirds in Region. Smaller size, drooping bill separate Dunlin from dowitchers (page 143).

Seasonal Abundance: Common migrant, winter resident in Region, arrives late in fall (mostly October). Attains breeding plumage by April, departs by early May. Breeds on tundra around northern hemisphere, winters south from temperate latitudes to subtropics.

Where to Find: Throughout lowlands; best bet Ankeny National Wildlife Refuge.

Habitat: Muddy fields, sewage ponds, lakes, reservoirs.

Diet and Behavior: Forages by picking, probing mud, primarily for aquatic organisms; may eat some plant material. Tight, swirling flocks move with mechanized precision, alternately flashing white, gray; large numbers in distance may appear to be smoke.

Voice: Flight call harsh *kreev*.

Did you know? Formerly known as Red-backed Sandpiper in reference to its bright spring color, the Dunlin derives its current name from the "dun" plumage it wears for most of the year.

Date and Location Seen: _____

Short-billed Dowitcher
Breeding

Short-billed Dowitcher
Juvenile

Long-billed Dowitcher
Breeding

Long-billed Dowitcher
Non-breeding

Description: 11". Stocky. **Long, straight bill, white wedge on back**, finely banded tail, greenish legs, mostly dark wings, **whitish eye-line. Rusty breast in breeding plumage**, overall grayish in winter. SHORT-BILLED: Summer–fall juvenile has **bright-golden markings near tip of folded wing**. LONG-BILLED: Underparts entirely rusty in breeding plumage (Short-billed has white belly).

Similar Species: Longer bill than similarly sized shorebirds except Wilson's Snipe (page 145) which has white stripes on head, back. Stilt Sandpiper (not shown; rare fall migrant in Region) smaller, proportionally longer-legged, often feeds with dowitchers.

Seasonal Abundance: SHORT-BILLED: Uncommon fall migrant in Region (late June–October), rare in spring. Breeds Canada, Alaska, winters to South America. LONG-BILLED: Fairly common migrant in Region, uncommon in winter. Breeds northwestern North America, northeastern Siberia, winters to Mexico.

Where to Find: Mostly lowlands. Short-billed usually found within flocks of Long-billed.

Habitat: Mudflats, marshes, pools, sewage ponds.

Diet and Behavior: Probe mud like sewing machine, primarily for aquatic organisms, also plant material. Usually flock, often with other shorebirds.

Voice: SHORT-BILLED: Low, liquid, whistled *tlu tu tu*, given in flight. LONG-BILLED: Sharp *keek*, sometimes in rapid series.

Did you know? The two species are difficult to separate. Bill length averages longer for Long-billed but there is much overlap.

Date and Location Seen: _____

Description: 10″. Stocky. Mostly brown with **long, straight bill**, short, greenish legs, dark wings, **rust-orange tail, white lower breast, belly**. Bold **whitish streaks on head, face, back**, dark bars along flanks.

Similar Species: Much longer bill than other similarly sized shorebirds except dowitchers (page 143), which lack white stripes on head, back.

Seasonal Abundance: Locally common winter resident in Region (July–May), uncommon in summer. Ranges across North America, winters to northern South America.

Where to Find: Throughout lowlands, up to moderate elevations.

Habitat: Wet ground including marshes, bogs, flooded fields, margins of ponds, streams.

Diet and Behavior: Forages mostly for insects, worms, other organisms by probing mud, shallow water. Sits tight, relying on camouflage until approached closely, then flushes explosively. Often concentrates in loose flocks during migration. Male flies high in breeding display, with shallow dives during which vibrating tail feathers produce hollow whinny sound ("winnowing").

Voice: Abrupt rasping *skresh* uttered when flushed. Breeding call *chip a*, repeated many times from exposed perch.

Did you know? The eyes of the Wilson's Snipe are set well back on the sides of the head, enabling it literally to watch its back for danger even as it probes for food.

Date and Location Seen: _____

Female Breeding

Juvenile

Description: 7¼". Small, **swimming shorebird** with straight, thin, black bill; white wing stripe visible in flight. BREEDING: Female with gray cap, white chin, reddish neck, gold-striped back, gray sides, white belly. Male similar but duller. NON-BREEDING: Gray-and-white-striped above, plain white below, with dark cap, **thick, dark line behind eye**. JUVENILE: Resembles adult non-breeding; early juveniles have gold-striped back.

Similar Species: Wilson's Phalarope (not shown; rare in Region): dark stripe extends from bill down side of neck, no wing stripe; more likely on land.

Seasonal Abundance: Fairly common fall migrant in Region, late July–October (juveniles, non-breeding-plumaged adults); less common spring migrant, mostly May (breeding-plumaged birds). Breeds on tundra at low latitudes around northern hemisphere, winters in tropical oceans. Migrates primarily at sea.

Where to Find: Widespread, usually with other shorebird species.

Habitat: Sewage ponds, lakes, flooded farm fields.

Diet and Behavior: Feeds on open water while swimming, often in circles, picking insects, other small organisms from surface. Seldom occurs on land except while nesting.

Voice: Frequent *kit kit* call.

Did you know? The usual sexual roles are reversed in phalaropes, with the smaller, duller-plumaged male incubating the eggs and raising the young.

Date and Location Seen: _____

Breeding

Non-breeding

First-year

Description: 13″, wingspan 32″. **Petite** gull; transitions to full adult plumage over two years. White below, pearl-gray back, black bill, short red legs. Square tail, **upper surface of forewing white**, outer trailing edge black. BREEDING: **Head black**. NON-BREEDING: **Head white with black spot behind eye**. FIRST-YEAR: Black tail tip, wing pattern.

Similar Species: Common, Forster's Terns (not shown; rare migrants in Region) have strongly forked tail, black limited to cap. Franklin's Gull (not shown; rare in Region) larger with darker back; juveniles, non-breeding-plumaged birds show dark half-hood.

Seasonal Abundance: Uncommon migrant in Region (October–November, March–April), rare in winter; numbers variable year to year. Breeds northern North America, winters to Mexico.

Where to Find: Throughout lowlands, usually flying over open bodies of water — e.g., Fern Ridge Reservoir, Sturgeon Lake (Sauvie Island). Rarely at higher elevations.

Habitat: Large lakes, reservoirs, sewage lagoons.

Diet and Behavior: Tern-like in flight. Forages for small fish, crustaceans, insects by plunge-diving or picking at water surface. Concentrates, occasionally in flocks of hundreds, at sewage ponds.

Voice: Call unlike that of most gulls — low, harsh, grating *geerr*.

Did you know? Bonaparte's Gulls build their nests in coniferous trees in the boreal forests of Alaska and Canada.

Date and Location Seen: _____

Breeding

Non-breeding

First-year

Description: 15", wingspan 43". Small gull; transitions to full adult plumage over three years. BREEDING: Tail, underparts white; back light-slaty-gray. White, **dove-like head, short yellowish bill, dark eye**, yellow legs. **Wingtips black with large white spots** near tip. NON-BREEDING: Head heavily streaked. FIRST-YEAR: Streaky brown with gray back, pink legs, dark eye, dark-tipped bill.

Similar Species: Smaller than most gulls in Region. Adult darker gray, more white in wingtips than Ring-billed (page 153).

Seasonal Abundance: Common winter resident in Region, arrives beginning in August, leaves by May. Breeds Alaska, northwestern Canada, winters southern Alaska to Baja California along Pacific Coast. Several other races in Eurasia.

Where to Find: Lowlands, mainly at north end of Willamette Valley.

Habitat: Agricultural fields, golf courses, sewage ponds.

Diet and Behavior: Omnivorous; forages for worms in plowed fields; fish, marine organisms along waterways; insect larvae, waste in sewage ponds. May flycatch during insect hatches. Gregarious; often flocks with other gulls, especially Ring-billeds.

Voice: Calls higher than those of other gulls, with mewed quality.

Did you know? Most gulls breed in colonies and are highly gregarious outside the nesting season. This enables information-sharing, which is important for birds dependent on locally abundant but unpredictable food sources.

Date and Location Seen: _____

Non-breeding

First-year

Description: 17", wingspan 46". **Medium-sized** gull; transitions to full adult plumage over three years. BREEDING: Pearl-gray back, white head, underparts, tail; **wingtips extensively black** with white spot near tip. **Yellow bill with black ring near tip,** yellow eye, legs. NON-BREEDING: Head streaked. FIRST-YEAR: Gray back, whitish underparts lightly scalloped with brown, dark eye, pink legs, dark-tipped bill.

Similar Species: Larger gulls have heavier bills. Adult Mew Gull (page 151) has smaller bill, darker back, whiter wingtips.

Seasonal Abundance: Common migrant, winter resident in Region; uncommon in summer but does not nest. Ranges from southeastern Alaska to Labrador, south to Mexico, Caribbean.

Where to Find: Throughout lowlands, rare at higher elevations.

Habitat: Agricultural fields, lakes, reservoirs, sewage ponds; urban settings including parking lots.

Diet and Behavior: Omnivorous. Forages widely for fish; worms in plowed fields; refuse, scraps in cities. Often flycatches during insect hatches, steals food from other birds. Long-lived, colonial nester with elaborate courtship, complex social behaviors. Gregarious, often flocks with other gulls.

Voice: Typical gull calls including long sequence of laugh-like squeals, beginning with long calls then trailing to shorter ones.

Did you know? Other gull species may have rings on their bills during winter and in transitional plumages. Take care not to confuse them with Ring-billed Gulls.

Date and Location Seen: _____

Breeding

First-year

Description: 20", wingspan 53". Fairly large gull; transitions to full adult plumage over four years. BREEDING: White head, underparts, tail; **light-slaty-gray back; wingtips black** with white near tip. Dark eye, **greenish-yellow legs**, fairly thin **bill with black-and-red spot near tip**. NON-BREEDING: Head streaked, legs greener. FIRST-YEAR: Streaky dark-brown with some gray feathering (variable); pink legs, two-toned bill.

Similar Species: Only adult gull in Region with yellowish legs, black-and-red spot on bill.

Seasonal Abundance: Uncommon winter–spring in Region, becomes fairly common by summer, locally common late summer–fall as migrants arrive from breeding colonies in eastern Oregon, Great Plains. Breeds interior western North America, winters coastally British Columbia–Mexico.

Where to Find: Primarily lowlands, but may be seen flying west over mountain passes in summer.

Habitat: Agricultural lands, ponds, lakes, rivers, city parks, golf courses.

Diet and Behavior: Forages for fish, carrion along waterways; in plowed fields for rodents, worms; in city refuse. May flycatch, steal food from other birds. Often flocks with other gulls.

Voice: Typical for gull; can be harsh.

Did you know? California Gulls rescued Mormon settlers at the Great Salt Lake from the grasshopper plague of 1848.

Date and Location Seen: _____

Non-breeding

First-year

Description: 24", wingspan 57". Medium-large gull; transitions to full adult plumage over four years. BREEDING: Underparts, tail white, back **light-gray, wingtips black with white tips**. Sloping forehead, relatively small, straight **bill with red spot** near tip, **pale-yellow eye**, pink legs. NON-BREEDING: Head heavily streaked. FIRST-YEAR: Variably mottled dark-brown with lighter head; eye dark, bill dark or two-toned.

Similar Species: Adult Thayer's Gull (page 159) has rounder head, wingtips blackish above but grayish below; most have dark eye. California Gull (page 155) adult with greenish-yellow legs. Hybrid Glaucous-winged × Western Gull (page 161) bill heavier, more angular.

Seasonal Abundance: Fairly common resident in Region, October–April. Breeds around northern hemisphere, winters to tropics.

Where to Find: Most common in lowlands near Portland, Eugene, but widely scattered throughout Region.

Habitat: Near water; also landfills, urban areas, agricultural fields, golf courses, parking lots.

Diet and Behavior: Omnivorous, forages mostly for fish, invertebrates, carrion, refuse. Often flocks with other gulls.

Voice: Typical for gull.

Did you know? In spring, large numbers of Herring Gulls, and other gulls, gather along the Columbia River for the annual smelt runs.

Date and Location Seen: _____

Non-breeding

First-year

Description: 23", wingspan 55". Medium-large gull; transitions to full adult plumage over four years. BREEDING: Underparts, tail white, gray back, **wingtips appear all-gray from below** but blackish with white tips from above. Round head, **dark eye** (pale in small percentage), **small bill** with red spot, **legs bright-pink**. NON-BREEDING: Head heavily streaked. FIRST-YEAR: Variably mottled brown, darker wingtips edged white, bill black.

Similar Species: Dark wingtips of other gulls apparent from below as well as from above. Herring Gull (page 157) adult has yellow eye. Adult California Gull (page 155) has greenish-yellow legs. Hybrid Glaucous-winged × Western Gull (page 161) bill much heavier, forehead sloping.

Seasonal Abundance: Fairly common winter resident in Region, arrives by October, departs March. Breeds in central Canadian Arctic; most winter along Pacific Coast, southeast Alaska–Baja California.

Where to Find: Widespread, but most regular in Portland metropolitan area.

Habitat: Agricultural lands, golf courses, city parks.

Diet and Behavior: Omnivorous. Forages mostly for fish, mollusks, carrion, urban refuse. Gregarious, often flocking with other gulls.

Voice: Typical for gull.

Did you know? Thayer's Gull is sought after by visiting birders due to its relative abundance in the Region.

Date and Location Seen: _____

Western Gull

Breeding

First-year

Description: 25", wingspan 58". Large gull; transitions to full adult plumage over four years. BREEDING: White head, underparts, tail, pearl-gray back; **wingtips same gray as back**, white spots near tip. **Massive yellow bill** with red spot near tip, **pink legs**. NON-BREEDING: Head streaked. FIRST-YEAR: Rather uniform brownish or grayish, including wingtips; bill black.

Similar Species: Most gulls smaller with smaller bills; other large gulls have dark wingtips, except Glaucous Gull (not shown; rare in Region) which has white wingtips.

Seasonal Abundance: Common migrant, winter resident in Region; uncommon summer, rarely breeds. Range coastal (Alaska–Mexico).

Where to Find: Widespread, may be seen anywhere.

Habitat: Rivers, lakes, agricultural fields, golf courses, cities.

Diet and Behavior: Omnivorous, opportunistic. Forages on land, water for fish, mollusks, carrion, refuse in cities, worms in fields. Gregarious, flocking with other gulls.

Voice: Calls, typical for gull, include sequences of laugh-like bugling, staccato *ca ca ca* given in alarm.

Did you know? Glaucous-winged Gull hybridizes with the more southerly **Western Gull** (see inset; uncommon in Region), which is **dark-gray** above with **black wingtips**. The resulting offspring are intermediate in plumage. Most "Glaucous-wingeds" in the Willamette Valley Region are actually hybrids, with wingtips a shade darker than the back.

Date and Location Seen: _____

Breeding

Description: 20", wingspan 48". Stocky tern, white below, pearl-gray back with large, **thick red bill, black cap**, whitish, shallowly forked tail, **long, pointed wings** with dark tips on undersurface. NON-BREEDING: Whitish forehead. FIRST-YEAR: Whitish forehead, back mottled with brown.

Similar Species: Other terns much smaller, with thin bills. Gulls lack red bill.

Seasonal Abundance: Fairly common summer resident in Region (April–September), but does not nest. Ranges nearly worldwide in temperate, tropical zones.

Where to Find: Widespread; most regular along Columbia River (e.g., Sauvie Island). Large nesting colony on East Sand Island near Columbia mouth, just outside Region.

Habitat: Rivers, lakes, open shorelines, mudflats.

Diet and Behavior: Forages fairly high over water, plunge-dives for small fish, often several feet below surface; also picks fish off surface.

Voice: Often heard before seen. Common call low, harsh, screeching *kaa yarrr*. Juveniles beg with whistled *wheee oo*.

Did you know? Caspian Terns have recently come into conflict with fisheries management goals due to their skill at catching salmon smolts swimming downriver to the sea from the hatcheries where they were reared.

Date and Location Seen: _____

Breeding

Description: 9½″, wingspan 24″. **Petite** tern with buoyant flight. Slightly forked tail appears square when spread. BREEDING: **Head, underparts black**; back, wings, tail gray; undertail white; legs, short bill blackish. NON-BREEDING: White underparts, dark-gray back, cap, ear spot, partial collar. IMMATURE: Similar to non-breeding; back browner with buff edging, legs pinkish-orange.

Similar Species: Common, Forster's Terns (neither shown; both rare migrants in Region) larger with forked tails, white underparts. Bonaparte's Gull (page 149) larger, white below.

Seasonal Abundance: Locally fairly common in Region May–September. Small nesting population; transients swell numbers during late spring. Breeds in temperate latitudes across North America, Europe, western Asia, winters to tropics.

Where to Find: Wetlands mainly in southern part of Region. Has nested at Baskett Slough, Ridgefield National Wildlife Refuges, Fern Ridge Reservoir.

Habitat: Marshes, lakes, ponds, wet meadows, flooded fields.

Diet and Behavior: Forages mostly on insects, some small fish, invertebrates, coursing over wetlands, water surface in erratic, dipping flight, skimming from water surface. Loosely colonial breeder, gregarious year round.

Voice: Peeping, harsh *kreef*.

Did you know? Black Terns nest abundantly east of the Cascades. Small breeding colonies established recently in the Willamette Valley appear to be increasing.

Date and Location Seen: _____

Description: 13", wingspan 28". Familiar domestic pigeon, **highly variable in color, patterning**. Most common form gray with **dark bill**, flesh-colored legs, dark head, neck; iridescent feathers on neck, two black bars across wing, **black band at tip of tail. White rump, underwing** visible in flight.

Similar Species: Band-tailed Pigeon (page 169) has yellow bill with black tip; gray, not white rump, white on nape of neck, broad gray band on tail, yellow legs, dark underwing.

Seasonal Abundance: Common, widespread year-round resident in Region. Native to Old World; domesticated birds introduced, now naturalized essentially worldwide.

Where to Find: City parks, streets, industrial zones; bridges, overpasses; rural seed fields, barns, grain elevators.

Habitat: Lowlands. Cities, towns, rural settings near human habitation.

Diet and Behavior: Forages mostly on ground for grain, seeds, grasses, food scraps. Feeds, travels in flocks. Flies at speeds up to 85 miles per hour — one of fastest birds in Region.

Voice: Soft cooing.

Did you know? Introduced by early European settlers, the Rock Pigeon is now widespread throughout North America and one of the most abundant urban birds, building nests on window ledges, water towers, bridges, and other structures.

Date and Location Seen: _____

Description: 14″, wingspan 26″. Overall gray with purplish head, breast, **black-tipped yellow bill, gray rump, pale-gray band on tail, yellow legs**, white bar above iridescent feathers on nape (absent in juveniles). **Dark underwing** visible in flight.

Similar Species: Rock Pigeon (page 167) has white, not gray, rump, flesh-colored legs, all-dark bill, white underwing.

Seasonal Abundance: Fairly common summer resident in Region, uncommon in winter; most go south September–October, return beginning late February. Ranges from southwestern British Columbia, Colorado, to Argentina.

Where to Find: Well-treed neighborhoods, parks, forests, e.g., Mount Tabor Park (Portland), Pigeon Butte (Finley National Wildlife Refuge).

Habitat: Breeds low-elevation coniferous, mixed forests; uncommon to mountain passes. Prefers tall conifers, forest edges with nearby open spaces. Post-breeders, migrants regular in mountains.

Diet and Behavior: Feeds mostly on nuts, seeds, fruits of deciduous trees, shrubs such as oak, cherry, elderberry, madrone, cascara. Attracted to feeders with black-oil sunflower, cracked corn, millet. Visits mineral springs. Usually forages, travels in small flocks. When taking flight, wings produce loud clapping noise.

Voice: Low, repetitive *whoo oo whoo*.

Did you know? The cooing of the Band-tailed Pigeon is often mistaken for that of an owl.

Date and Location Seen: _____

Description: 12", wingspan 18". **Slender**; mostly tan-colored with **long, pointed tail**, black spots on pointed wings, flesh-colored legs. Male has pinkish hue to breast, blue crown. **Bill small, thin, black**. White tips of outer tail feathers visible in flight.

Similar Species: Band-tailed Pigeon (page 169), typical Rock Pigeon (page 167) gray, considerably heavier-bodied, tail proportionally shorter.

Seasonal Abundance: Fairly common resident in Region, some migrate south for winter.

Where to Find: Widespread in summer; winter concentration best at Sauvie Island.

Habitat: Lowlands. Mostly open habitats including grasslands (prairie, agricultural), recent clearcuts, semi-rural residential tracts, towns. Attracted to feeders.

Diet and Behavior: Mostly seeds, grains (sunflower seed, millet, cracked corn at feeders). Often seen on overhead wires. Picks up gravel along railroad tracks, roadsides to help grind food. In winter, forms flocks at sites with plentiful food, nearby trees for sheltering, roosting. Wings whistle when taking flight.

Voice: Slow, mournful cooing, *ooo aaa ooo ooo ooo*.

Did you know? The Passenger Pigeon, driven to extinction in the 19th century, was once the most widespread, common, and prolific member of the pigeon/dove family in North America — a distinction now held by its close relative, the Mourning Dove.

Date and Location Seen: _____

Description: 15″, wingspan 40″. **Slim, long-legged, round-headed owl** with prominent **heart-shaped facial disc**, dark-brown eyes, long, yellowish, hooked bill. Brownish-tan back with pearl-gray spots, mostly white underparts impart **pale appearance**. In flight, tail looks fairly long, wings appear bowed.

Similar Species: Barred Owl (page 179) bulkier, broader winged. Short-eared Owl (page 181) has floppier flight, dark wing patches.

Seasonal Abundance: Fairly common resident in Region. Ranges worldwide in temperate, tropical zones.

Where to Find: Lowlands, including cities.

Habitat: Open areas: farmland, fields, wetlands, clearcuts, urban landscapes with buildings, trees for day-roosting.

Diet and Behavior: Extremely nocturnal. Hunts from perches or in low flight by sight, sound, captures prey in talons. Directional hearing well-developed for locating rodents, its primary quarry, in high grass. Also takes some birds, insects, cold-blooded animals. Roosts in buildings or dense conifers by day. Does not build nest; lays up to 10 eggs in dark corner of building, large nest box, cave, tree cavity.

Voice: Varied calls include harsh, grating screech, long hiss, series of metallic clicks.

Did you know? One Barn Owl can eat over 1,500 mice per year.

Date and Location Seen: _____

Description: 7½". **Small** but robust, mottled grayish or brownish, **block-headed** with **prominent ear tufts** (sometimes held flat), **yellow eyes**. Breast, belly streaked, finely barred.

Similar Species: Combination of small size, ear tufts, yellow eyes eliminates other owls.

Seasonal Abundance: Fairly common resident in Region. Ranges across West, southeastern Alaska to Mexico.

Where to Find: Widespread, but may be absent in suitable-looking habitat. Most often found in streamside woodlands at lower elevations.

Habitat: Broadleaf, mixed woodlands, including forest edge, parks, backyards. Often along watercourses.

Diet and Behavior: Extremely nocturnal. Hunts from perches, swoops, captures prey in talons. Locates prey by sight, sound. Favors rodents, large insects, but will take birds, reptiles, amphibians. Does not build nest; uses existing tree cavities. Usually responds to imitations of its calls by approaching, calling to protect territory.

Voice: Common call accelerating series of low whistles in pattern of ball bouncing, then coming to rest (notes start far apart, higher, get progressively closer together, lower).

Did you know? Distributed throughout the New World, the more than 20 small, tufted owls of the genus *Megascops* are often closely similar. Researchers only recently concluded that Western and Eastern Screech-Owls were two separate species, based on differences in vocalizations.

Date and Location Seen: _____

Description: 22", wingspan 45". Formidable owl, mottled grayish-brown, **block-headed** with **prominent ear tufts. Yellow eyes**, brownish facial disc, **white throat**, finely barred lower breast, belly.

Similar Species: Long-eared Owl (not shown; rare in Region) also has prominent ear tufts, but smaller (15", one-fifth as heavy) with vertical streaks below.

Seasonal Abundance: Fairly common resident in countryside in Region, somewhat less common in cities (may increase with influx of fall transients). Ranges throughout New World, from Arctic to South America.

Where to Find: Lowlands to tree line, although uncommon in dense conifer forest.

Habitat: Adaptable. Woodlands, meadows, farmlands, city parks.

Diet and Behavior: Hunts mostly at night, watching, listening for prey from perch, then pursuing, capturing it with talons. Diet extremely varied, mostly small mammals but also birds, large insects, cold-blooded animals including fish. Does not build nest; uses snags, cavities, nests of other species, especially Red-tailed Hawk. One of earliest-nesting birds, lays eggs as early as January.

Voice: Common call deep *whoo whodoo whoo who*. Begging young give harsh shrieks.

Did you know? Great Horned Owls are powerful, fearless hunters. They have been recorded killing and eating animals as large as Great Blue Herons and skunks.

Date and Location Seen: _____

Spotted Owl

Description: 19", wingspan 42". Bulky, grayish, with **dark-brown eyes. Rounded head** with white lines in ring-like pattern above dark-bordered facial disc. Hooked bill yellowish, upperparts mottled, streaked. **Upper breast barred; lower breast, belly whitish with dark streaks**.

Similar Species: Spotted Owl (see inset; rare resident of mature forests in Region) **dark-brown; lower breast darker, mottled**, not streaked. Great Horned Owl (page 177) has ear tufts, yellow eyes. Barn Owl (page 173) slimmer.

Seasonal Abundance: Recent arrival in Region, now fairly common resident. Ranges throughout eastern U.S., across southern Canada, to Northwest.

Where to Find: Throughout Region including forest tracts, parks within cites.

Habitat: Wet mixed, broadleaf forests; prefers dense woods but may disperse in fall to more-urbanized settings.

Diet and Behavior: Mostly nocturnal. Hunts from perches; favors rodents, but eats other small mammals, birds, reptiles, amphibians, large insects. Does not build nest — uses large cavities, nests of other species. Vocal, territorial, occasionally even toward humans.

Voice: Loud hoots including *who cooks for you, who cooks for you allll* sequence.

Did you know? Barred Owls first reached Oregon in 1974 in the far northeastern corner of the state. They have now hybridized with, or replaced, the closely related Spotted Owl in many areas.

Date and Location Seen: _____

Description: 14″, wingspan 38″. **Moth-like flight** on long, broad wings. Streaked upperparts, upper breast, light below. In flight shows **dark patch near wrist**, buff patch toward outer end of upperwing. Yellow eyes, prominent facial disc; short ear tufts seldom visible.

Similar Species: Slow, floppy flight, daytime activity unlike other large owls in Region. Burrowing Owl (not shown; rare in Region) smaller with longer legs.

Seasonal Abundance: Fairly common winter resident in Region (October–April), but numbers vary year to year; uncommon in summer, may occasionally nest. Ranges through much of northern hemisphere, vacating northern parts in winter; also resident in South America.

Where to Find: Widespread in open habitat. Most regular Farmer Road (Baskett Slough National Wildlife Refuge), Fern Ridge Reservoir, Vancouver Lake bottomlands.

Habitat: Wet meadows, agricultural fields, marshes.

Diet and Behavior: Highly migratory, nomadic. Hunts low over fields, mostly near dawn, dusk, but may fly in full daylight. Locates small mammals, birds by sight, sound, often hovering before pouncing, capturing with talons. Concentrates in loose flocks at areas of prey abundance, roosts on ground by day.

Voice: Gives nasal barks, wheezy whistles when multiple birds hunt.

Did you know? Short-eared Owls nest on the ground. As many as ten young may leave a nest in as little as two weeks.

Date and Location Seen: _____

Juvenile

Description: 7". Small, **round-headed, yellow-eyed** owl, white below with broad, brown streaking, brown back, large white wing spots, **fine white streaks on face, head**. JUVENILE: Plain brown, ochre below, with white forehead.

Similar Species: Western Screech-Owl (page 175) larger, block-headed, with ear tufts (although these may be held flat). Northern Pygmy-Owl (page 377) smaller, with long tail, smaller head, typically active in daylight. Boreal Owl (not shown; limited to high mountains) rather similar but larger.

Seasonal Abundance: Fairly common resident in Region but seldom seen, numbers augmented in winter by migrants. Ranges across North America from southeast Alaska to eastern Maritimes, south in mountains to Mexico.

Where to Find: Sea level to mountain passes; scarce in urban areas.

Habitat: Coniferous, mixed woodlands, often near water.

Diet and Behavior: Extremely nocturnal. Locates prey by sight, sound; favors rodents, also takes birds, insects. Nests in tree cavities, habitually roosts in one spot in dense conifers where best located by resulting pile of feces. Strongly migratory; may move south or downslope in fall.

Voice: Calls include rhythmic tooting, *skews*, twitters, barks, whining whistles, may be elicited by imitating its tooting call.

Did you know? Emaciated Saw-whet Owls may appear near bird feeders in winter.

Date and Location Seen: _____

COMMON NIGHTHAWK
Chordeiles minor

Description: 9½", wingspan 24". Short-legged, relatively long-tailed, **mottled grayish-brown** above, banded brown below; **long, pointed, angular wings with conspicuous broad white band** near tip. **Usually seen high in flight**. Appears owl-like at rest; wingtips extend beyond tail-tip. MALE: White chin, tail band. FEMALE: Buffy chin.

Similar Species: Swallows, swifts much smaller; falcons have more direct flight, lack white wing bands.

Seasonal Abundance: Uncommon migrant, summer resident in Region (late May–early September). Highly migratory; breeds across most of North, Middle America, winters South America.

Where to Find: Nests in clearcuts, rarely rural lowlands; most often seen late summer in metropolitan areas.

Habitat: Open habitats: forest clearings, stony ground, weedy lots. Hunts, migrates over cities, forests, fields.

Diet and Behavior: Forages aerially with erratic flight — mostly near dawn, dusk, but active at any hour. Short bill opens to huge gape for catching insects. Perches lengthwise along branches. Nests on open ground, relying on camouflage. In courtship males dive steeply, producing booming sound.

Voice: Far-carrying nasal buzz given repeatedly in flight.

Did you know? Nighthawks belong to a group of birds called goatsuckers, which are most closely related to owls. Two other nighthawk species reach the southern United States.

Date and Location Seen: _____

Description: 4¾". Usually seen foraging high overhead on **pointed, curving wings** with rapid, **flickering wing-beats**, brief intervals of gliding. Darkish overall; **throat, breast, rump paler** than rest of plumage (hard to spot in field). Short tail tapers to point when closed, giving **"winged cigar"** look.

Similar Species: Black Swift (not shown; rare in Region) larger, with broader wingbase, longer tail (often notched). Wing-beat slower, shallower; glides frequently. Violet-green Swallow (page 245) may use similar aerial foraging strategy, flitting wing-beats; white underparts not always visible at distance, but wings proportionally shorter, broader, less swept-back.

Seasonal Abundance: Locally common resident in Region, May–September. Nests from southeastern Alaska through western Montana to California, winters in Mexico, Guatemala. Other races resident in Mexico, Central America, Venezuela.

Where to Find: Over coniferous forests in evening; nests in chimneys in suburban neighborhoods. Conspicuous late-summer evening roosts in chimneys, e.g., Chapman School (Portland), Agate Hall (Eugene).

Habitat: Nests widely in hollow trees, unused chimneys. Hunts opportunistically over water, forest, marshes.

Diet and Behavior: Small insects taken on wing.

Voice: Rapid, high-pitched chip notes.

Did you know? Vaux's Swifts perch vertically against the sides of trees or chimneys, using their stiff-spined tails for support. Their nest is a flimsy bunch of tiny twigs glued together with saliva.

Date and Location Seen: _____

Male

Female

Description: 4″. MALE: Green back, grayish underparts, **iridescent-red crown**, throat (can appear black in shadow), dark tail. FEMALE: Similar except outer tail feathers tipped white, red restricted to small spot on throat. IMMATURE: Little or no red.

Similar Species: Female/immature Rufous Hummingbirds (page 191) have rufous flanks, tail base, undertail.

Seasonal Abundance: Common year-round resident in Region; increasing, spreading. Original range along Pacific Coast from northern Baja California to San Francisco Bay; now breeds north to Vancouver Island, east to Arizona.

Where to Find: Lowlands, especially cities. Reliable at Mount Tabor Park (Portland).

Habitat: Human-influenced: parks, gardens, residential neighborhoods. Hummingbird feeders, exotic flowering plants may help account for phenomenally successful range extension.

Diet and Behavior: Consumes nectar from flowers, sugar-water from hummingbird feeders, sap from holes in trees (often drilled by woodpeckers), small insects, spiders. Can survive short bouts of severe cold weather by lowering body temperature at night, converting more sugar to fat, or entering torpor (dormancy).

Voice: Loud chip note. Song dry, rasping, delivered year round from exposed perch. Various squeaks, buzzes, chattering sounds in courtship, territorial defense.

Did you know? Male Anna's defend their territories with "dive displays", looping 60–120 feet into the air then zooming down to emit a loud pop in the intruder's face.

Date and Location Seen: _____

Male

Female

Description: 3¾". Bill straight, dark. MALE: **Back, tail, underparts rusty-orange**; back may have variable amounts of green. Crown green, upper breast white, throat iridescent-orange-red. FEMALE: Upperparts, crown green; **tail base, undertail, flanks rufous**; outer tail feathers white-tipped. Red feathering on throat varies from none up to small spot. JUVENILE: Resembles female.

Similar Species: Female/immature Anna's Hummingbirds (page 189) show no rufous coloration.

Seasonal Abundance: Common summer resident in Region. Breeds from northern California to western Montana, southern Alaska; winters in southern U.S., Mexico. Males arrive before females in spring, sometimes by late February.

Where to Find: Widespread throughout Region; most common in Coast Range where large numbers often besiege feeders.

Habitat: Forest openings, disturbed areas, brushy edges; lowlands in spring, moves up into flowering meadows in mountains as season progresses.

Diet and Behavior: Consumes nectar from flowers, sugar-water from hummingbird feeders, sap from holes in trees (often drilled by woodpeckers), small insects, spiders. Male has diving courtship display.

Voice: Chip, other warning notes. No song. Adult male's wings make high-pitched whine.

Did you know? Rufous Hummingbird is the northernmost representative of this largely tropical New World family. It is also the smallest bird in the Willamette Valley Region.

Date and Location Seen: _____

Male

Female

Description: 13". **Large head, unkempt crest, stout bill.** MALE: Mostly **slate-blue with white underparts, collar; wide slate-blue breastband**. FEMALE: Identical but with rufous flanks, additional rufous band across lower breast. JUVENILE: Single dark breast band, rufous flanks.

Similar Species: None in Region.

Seasonal Abundance: Common year-round resident in Region. Nests continent wide — below Arctic tundra, north of arid Southwest. Retreats from northernmost parts at freezeup; winters along Pacific Coast (Aleutians south), across most of U.S., throughout Mexico, Caribbean (a few farther south).

Where to Find: From sea level to tree line, any stretch of shore with good nest sites, fishing prospects has its pair of kingfishers.

Habitat: Along streams, lakes, ponds with clear, relatively still waters where it can see prey.

Diet and Behavior: Watches from perch over water, or hovers; plunges in shallow dive (less than two feet below surface), seizes prey in bill. Takes mostly fish, some insects, crustaceans, other animals. Digs nest burrows, usually 3–6 feet deep in banks.

Voice: Main call loud rattle, somewhat like sound of ratchet noisemaker toy, given all year (often in flight).

Did you know? A Belted Kingfisher returns to its perch with a freshly caught fish in its bill, beats it senseless against the perch, then swallows it headfirst.

Date and Location Seen: _____

Male

Description: 9". Tree-clinging behavior, chisel-like bill typical of woodpeckers. Black back, chest; belly, **rump, outer wing patches white**; flanks streaked black. **Clown-like face**; white forehead, chin; red crown; black face with contrasting **white eye**. FEMALE: Crown-front black.

Similar Species: Pileated Woodpecker (page 205) crested, much larger.

Seasonal Abundance: Fairly common resident in Region, becoming rare in northern part. Ranges down West Coast from southernmost central Washington (Klickitat County) through Central America to Colombia.

Where to Find: Lowland oak groves, suburbs, city parks, neighborhoods, e.g., George Fox College (Forest Grove). Not found north of Portland.

Habitat: Restricted to oak groves, mixed woodlots with oaks. In southern part of Region also in tanoak, prefers older trees with open understory.

Diet and Behavior: Noisy, conspicuous. Lives in cooperative groups with complex social system, combining efforts to excavate nest cavities in dead wood, gather acorns in fall, store in defended granary tree for use in winter, spring when fresh food scarce. Also eats other seeds, insects (flycatches, captures from ground, trees), drinks from sap wells, feeders.

Voice: Calls include whinnying, rattles, raucous *whakka whakka*.

Did you know? Social groups include up to 15 Acorn Woodpeckers, four males often mating with one or two females.

Date and Location Seen: _____

Juvenile

Description: 8½". Typical woodpecker tree-clinging behavior, undulating flight, chisel-like bill. Colorful. **Breast, head entirely red** except for faint white mustache mark; belly yellowish, back black with white mottling. Elongated **white patch across center of upperwing**. JUVENILE: Dark-brownish, molts to adult plumage by September.

Similar Species: Red-naped Sapsucker (not shown; rare in Region except at Cascade crest) has white facial lines, no red below throat. Much larger Pileated Woodpecker (page 205) crested, with small white patch closer to end of wing.

Seasonal Abundance: Fairly common resident in Region. Ranges down coast, southwest Alaska to Baja California.

Where to Find: Coniferous, mixed forests; in winter may use urban parks, backyards, small woodlots.

Habitat: Prefers cedar, hemlock, spruce-dominated forests, but also found in various mixed woods.

Diet and Behavior: Quietly drills evenly spaced small holes in live trees, revisiting these "wells" on regular foraging routes to drink sap, feed on insects attracted to sap, berries, tree tissues. Moves downslope below level of heavy snow in winter. Excavates nest hole in conifer snag, aspen, or other soft wood.

Voice: Calls include nasal mews, squeals; territorial drumming irregularly spaced.

Did you know? Red-breasted Sapsucker interbreeds with the closely related Red-naped Sapsucker at the Cascade crest, resulting in intermediate-plumaged hybrids.

Date and Location Seen: _____

Male   Female

Description: 6¾". **Short, chisel-like bill**, stiff tail, tree-clinging behavior. **Dingy-white or buffy back**, underparts, eyebrow, mustache mark; black bars on white outer tail feathers; **wings checkered black-and-white**. MALE: Red spot at back of head. JUVENILE: Red on top of head.

Similar Species: Hairy Woodpecker (page 201) identical but larger, with bill as long as distance from back of head to bill base (Downy's bill only half this measurement).

Seasonal Abundance: Common lowland resident in Region, becoming uncommon at higher elevations. Ranges from Alaska to Labrador, south to Florida, Texas, California.

Where to Find: Woodlands, parks, neighborhoods, stream corridors, semi-open rural habitats, mostly at low elevations.

Habitat: Prefers broadleaf woods, but also found in mixed forests, hedgerows, thickets.

Diet and Behavior: Probes dead limbs, small twigs, weed stalks in search of insects, also feeds on fruits, seeds. Excavates nest cavity in dead wood; calls, drums to establish territory. Common at suet feeders. Flight undulating, like that of other woodpeckers.

Voice: Calls include rattle-like whinny, flat *pik* (not as sharp as that given by Hairy Woodpecker).

Did you know? Male and female Downy Woodpeckers often maintain separate feeding territories in winter.

Date and Location Seen: _____

Male   Female

Description: 9½". **Long chisel-like bill**, stiff tail, tree-clinging behavior. **Dingy-white back**, underparts, eyebrow, mustache mark, outer tail feathers; **wings checkered black-and-white**. MALE: Red spot at back of head. JUVENILE: Red on top of head.

Similar Species: Downy Woodpecker (page 199) identical but smaller, shorter-billed, with black spots on outer tail (juvenile Hairy may also show these).

Seasonal Abundance: Fairly common resident in Region. Ranges from Alaska to Labrador, south to Central America, Caribbean.

Where to Find: Throughout Region although scarce in urban areas.

Habitat: Prefers coniferous forest, but also uses mixed, broadleaf woods.

Diet and Behavior: Excavates dead wood, scrapes bark, probes in search of insects; may also feed on fruits, seeds, sap. Digs nest cavities in live or dead wood; drums, calls to establish territory. Regular at bird feeders. Flight undulating, like that of other woodpeckers.

Voice: Calls include *pik krrreeeeer*, very sharp *piik* (louder than similar call given by Downy Woodpecker).

Did you know? Hairy Woodpeckers resident west of the Cascades are dingy-white. In winter, small numbers of bright-white birds descend from the mountains to western Oregon lowlands.

Date and Location Seen: _____

Red-shafted
Male

Yellow-shafted
Male

Red-shafted
Female

Description: 12″. Robust, colorful, with **black crescent bib, white rump**. Long bill, stiff tail, tree-clinging behavior. Barred brown above, spotted buff below, with **brightly colored feather shafts**, most notable in wings. Two forms. RED-SHAFTED: Brown cap, gray face, **red shafts**, male with red mustache mark. YELLOW-SHAFTED: Gray cap, brown face, **yellow shafts, red crescent on nape**, male with black mustache mark.

Similar Species: Distinctive in Region.

Seasonal Abundance: Common resident in Region but highly migratory. Ranges throughout North America, Central America, Caribbean. Yellow-shafted, Red-shafted forms interbreed where ranges overlap along eastern slope of Rocky Mountains.

Where to Find: Throughout Region.

Habitat: Open woodlands, any semi-open area, urban woodlots, lawns.

Diet and Behavior: Forages on ground for ants, in trees for fruits, occasionally seeds where available. Loud calling, drumming, boisterous interactions, ability to thrive in urban areas make it noticeable. Excavates cavity nest in live or dead wood. Flight undulating, like that of other woodpeckers. Flocks in migration.

Voice: Calls include *woika woika woika*, long series of repeated *kuk* notes, piercing *keeww*.

Did you know? The red-shafted form resides year-round in the Region. Yellow-shafted birds are present fall to spring along with intergrades that show mixed characteristics.

Date and Location Seen: _____

Male

PILEATED WOODPECKER
Dryocopus pileatus

Description: 16". Chisel-like bill, stiff tail, tree-clinging behavior, undulating flight typical of woodpeckers. **Large**, lanky; **black** except for **large crimson crest, white neck stripe**, facial markings, underwings, wing patch. MALE: Red mustache mark.

Similar Species: Much larger than other woodpeckers in Region. Red, white markings, undulating flight distinguish it from crows.

Seasonal Abundance: Fairly common resident in Region. Ranges across southern Canada, U.S., except for most of interior West.

Where to Find: Throughout Region, including forest tracts, parks within urban areas; regularly seen in Portland's Forest Park, adjacent neighborhoods.

Habitat: Mature coniferous, mixed forests.

Diet and Behavior: Excavates large, deep, oval or rectangular holes in trees in search of insects, primarily ants. Chisels through hard wood to access insect-damaged tree centers. Also feeds on small fruits. Sometimes loud, obvious with tapping, banging, calling, but also secretive, hiding behind tree trunks. Often calls while flying above or within canopy.

Voice: Series of 10–15 wild-sounding *kuk* notes with irregular rhythm, abrupt ending. Territorial drumming slow, loud.

Did you know? With the probable extinction of the Ivory-billed Woodpecker of the southeastern United States and Cuba and the Imperial Woodpecker of Mexico, the Pileated Woodpecker is the largest member of the woodpecker family on the North American continent.

Date and Location Seen: _____

OLIVE-SIDED FLYCATCHER
Contopus cooperi

Description: 7½". **Upright stance**, dark-grayish-olive above, below, with wide white line extending from throat down chest to belly giving **vested appearance. Large head** with slight crest, long dark bill, **short tail**, impart stout profile. White rump tufts seldom visible.

Similar Species: Western Wood-Pewee (page 209) smaller, appears less vested, with smaller bill.

Seasonal Abundance: Fairly common May–September resident in Region, with migration, dispersal continuing throughout summer. Breeds from Alaska to Labrador, south in western mountains to New Mexico; winters to South America.

Where to Find: Throughout Region, but uncommon nester in lowlands.

Habitat: Fairly mature coniferous forest; prefers tree stands interspersed with open areas, including clearcuts, old burns, bogs.

Diet and Behavior: Makes wide-ranging sallies for large flying insects from exposed perch at top of tree or snag. Usually returns to perch in same spot. Calls frequently; best located by voice.

Voice: Calls include whistled *quick three beers* with second syllable strongly accented, also *pep pep pep* repeated at short intervals.

Did you know? The Olive-sided Flycatcher is declining in numbers, especially in the East. Suggested causes include tropical habitat loss and a reduction in prey availability.

Date and Location Seen: _____

Description: 6″. **Upright stance**, dark-olive-gray above, long wings with light-colored wing-bars, dusky chest, pale-yellowish belly. Slim with **fairly prominent crest**, dark bill with lighter base, **no eye-ring**.

Similar Species: More crested, but easily confused with smaller, lighter *Empidonax* flycatchers (pages 211–215). Olive-side Flycatcher (page 207) larger with shorter tail, larger head, more vested appearance.

Seasonal Abundance: Fairly common resident in Region from mid-May to mid-September. Breeds in West from Alaska south in mountains to Honduras, winters in South America.

Where to Find: Mostly lowlands but occurs to mountain passes. Seldom nests within urban areas but widespread in migration.

Habitat: Open woodlands, woodland edge, preferring broadleaf growth along water courses.

Diet and Behavior: Forages from exposed perch in tall shrub or tree, making sallies to capture insects; may return to same spot. Often flutters wings while perching. Calls throughout day in spring, early summer, so best located by voice.

Voice: Most frequent call burry, nasal *prreeer*. Song, given at dawn, combination of tones similar to call.

Did you know? Western Wood-Pewees build their nests on the horizontal surface of limbs, usually at a fork.

Date and Location Seen: _____

Description: 5½". Fairly distinctive member of look-alike Empidonax flycatcher group. **Upright stance**; olive-brown above, buff-white wing-bars, whitish underparts. **Appears slim**, fairly long, with **long, broad, pale bill. Eye-ring minimal or absent**.

Similar Species: Other *Empidonax* flycatchers in Region have prominent eye-rings. Western Wood-Pewee (page 209) slightly larger, much darker overall with more crested appearance.

Seasonal Abundance: Uncommon resident in Region, mid-May to September. Ranges across continent from extreme southern Canada south to California, Georgia; winters from Mexico to Panama.

Where to Find: Mostly at lower elevation, but also up to mountain passes in clearcuts. Nests within urban areas in appropriate habitat, scarce in migration away from nesting locations.

Habitat: Open, shrubby, wetland habitats, clearcuts, brushy forest edge.

Diet and Behavior: Forages from perch usually within tall shrub, making sallies to capture insects. Eats some berries in summer, fall. Easily located by voice: distinctive song given throughout day, but especially near dawn.

Voice: Harsh *fitz bew* song, with first syllable strongly accented. Calls include clear *whit*, buzzy *breet*.

Did you know? Identification of *Empidonax* flycatchers is notoriously difficult. The Alder Flycatcher — a close relative of the Willow Flycatcher that breeds farther north — is so similar that the two can be told apart only by their vocalizations.

Date and Location Seen: _____

Description: 5″. Difficult-to-identify member of look-alike *Empidonax* flycatcher group. **Upright stance; appears dark, large-headed**, long-winged. Grayish-green with wing-bars, yellowish wash on belly, **dusky-gray chest**, gray head with distinct eye-ring. Short bill may appear all-dark.

Similar Species: Pacific-slope Flycatcher (page 215) slimmer, brighter, eye-ring more asymmetrical. Willow Flycatcher (page 211) without eye-ring. Dusky Flycatcher (not shown; uncommon in Region) difficult to separate: longer tail, shorter wings, *whit* call. Western Wood-Pewee (page 209) larger, no eye-ring.

Seasonal Abundance: Fairly common resident in Region, mid-April to September. Breeds in West, Alaska to New Mexico; winters in highlands from southeastern Arizona to Honduras.

Where to Find: Nests in older coniferous forests throughout Region, away from urban areas. Most easily found from middle elevations to mountain passes. Widespread in migration.

Habitat: Prefers dense coniferous forests but also uses mixed woods, broadleaf thickets in migration.

Diet and Behavior: Sallies for insects from perch, frequently high in tree. Often flicks tail, wings nervously.

Voice: Song consists of several phrases including burry, distinctive *bureek*. Calls include sharp *peet*.

Did you know? Hammond's Flycatchers molt into fresh plumage before migrating south — unlike Dusky Flycatchers, which appear worn and faded in fall.

Date and Location Seen: _____

Description: 5¼". Fairly distinctive member of look-alike Empidonax flycatcher group. **Upright stance**; olive-green with wing-bars, yellow wash on underparts extends up to throat. Wide, **pale bill, slightly crested appearance**; strong, **asymmetrical eye-ring**, elongated behind eye.

Similar Species: Other *Empidonax* flycatchers in Region less yellow on upper breast, throat, with less prominent, more symmetrical eye-ring. Smaller, lighter-colored than Western Wood-Pewee (page 209).

Seasonal Abundance: Common resident in Region, mid-April–September. Breeds from southeastern Alaska south through Pacific states to Baja California, winters in Mexico.

Where to Find: Nests throughout Region from lowlands to mountain passes, including smaller wooded tracts within urban areas. Migrants also use thickets in parks, neighborhoods.

Habitat: Shaded interior of moist, mixed or coniferous forests, preferably with broadleaf understory.

Diet and Behavior: Forages by watching for insects while perched within leafy growth, then sallies to capture prey; stays close to cover. Difficult to see, but easily located by distinctive call. May eat some berries, especially in late summer.

Voice: High-pitched, rising, slurred *suweeet* call; three-part song of thin, squeaky notes heard less frequently.

Did you know? Pacific-slope Flycatcher is distinguishable only by call from the closely related Cordilleran Flycatcher of the interior West.

Date and Location Seen: _____

Black Phoebe

Say's Phoebe

Description: 6¾" / 7½". Typical flycatchers, **upright stance**, thin bill, **frequently dip tail**. BLACK: **Dull-black**, white belly, slightly crested, thin white tail edging. SAY'S: Grayish-brown with **cinnamon-buff belly, undertail**.

Similar Species: BLACK: Slate-colored Junco (page 341) grayer, prominent white outer tail. SAY'S: Western Kingbird (page 219) larger, yellow below. Female bluebirds (pages 279, 381) longer-tailed, thin whitish eyering, some bluish feathers.

Seasonal Abundance: Uncommon to rare in Region. BLACK: Local resident at south end of Willamette Valley, rare northward. Ranges from southwestern U.S. to Argentina. SAY'S: Transient February–April, rare at other seasons. Breeds in interior West from Alaska to Mexico, winters south to Mexico.

Where to Find: BLACK: Mostly lowlands, also to foothills. SAY'S: Mostly lowlands, but migrants have appeared above tree line.

Habitat: BLACK: Sheltered spots near slow-moving water. SAY'S: Open areas, pasture, roadsides; not linked to water.

Diet and Behavior: Sally from perch to catch insects. Nest in rock crevices, vacant buildings, under bridges, other sheltered places.

Voice: BLACK: Two-part, high whistle, rich chip. SAY'S: Lower-pitched whistles.

Did you know? The Black Phoebe has extended its range in recent years, reaching the Willamette Valley as a breeding bird during the 1990s; a few now winter north to the Columbia River.

Date and Location Seen: _____

Western Kingbird

Eastern Kingbird

WESTERN KINGBIRD / EASTERN KINGBIRD
Tyrannus verticalis / Tyrannus tyrannus

Description: 8½". Large-headed with **upright stance**, square-tipped, fairly long tail, pointed black bill. WESTERN: Grayish upper breast, y**ellow belly**, greenish-gray back, **black tail with white edges**. EASTERN: **White below**, gray above with **white tail tip**.

Similar Species: Olive-Sided Flycatcher (page 207) smaller with short tail, vested appearance. Say's Phoebe (page 217) smaller, lacks white underparts, tail edging.

Seasonal Abundance: WESTERN: Uncommon summer resident in Region, late May–August. Breeds western North America from southern Canada to northern Mexico, winters southern Mexico to Costa Rica. EASTERN: Rare migrant in Region, nests regularly at Sandy River delta. Breeds from Washington, British Columbia across North America, south to Texas, Florida; winters in western Amazon Basin.

Where to Find: Lowlands. Western may appear anywhere in open areas, Eastern mostly at Sandy River delta nesting site.

Habitat: Fields, open rural areas with trees, structures for nesting, often near water.

Diet and Behavior: Forage from prominent perches, flying out to capture insects; also eat fruit.

Voice: Vocal at nest. WESTERN: Call sharp *kit*; transients seldom call. EASTERN: Rapid twittering notes.

Did you know? Both species are aggressive toward intruders near their nests, often attacking much larger birds.

Date and Location Seen: _____

Description: 9½″. Large-headed, long-tailed songbird, mostly pearl-gray; **wings, tail, mask black**, rump white. **White marks in wing, outer tail visible in flight. Bill large** with slight hook. Immature browner, dark markings less distinct; scaling below.

Similar Species: Loggerhead Shrike (not shown; rare in Region) smaller, darker, with heavier mask that crosses over base of smaller bill.

Seasonal Abundance: Uncommon resident in Region, October to early April. Breeds on tundra around northern hemisphere, winters to temperate zone.

Where to Find: Lowlands to lower foothills; migrants may appear in open areas within cities.

Habitat: Fields, agricultural areas, other open places with scattered trees, bushes.

Diet and Behavior: Preys on small mammals, birds, insects by perching prominently, often at highest point of shrub, then swooping down, dispatching victim with bill. Often impales food on thorn or barbed wire in sheltered location to facilitate feeding or store for later use. Flight slightly undulating with rapid flapping, halting pauses.

Voice: Occasionally offers mellow, warbled phrases of song in winter quarters. Mimics songs of other bird species.

Did you know? Northern Shrikes, often called butcher birds, appear in variable numbers each winter dependent on reproductive success and food supply in the far north.

Date and Location Seen: _____

Description: 5½". Compact with short tail, heavy bill. Grayish-green above with **grayer head**, white below with yellowish flanks. Prominent **white wing-bars, bold well-defined white spectacles**.

Similar Species: Hutton's Vireo (page 225) smaller with diffuse white eye-ring. Other vireos lack wing-bars. Red-eyed Vireo (page 229) song somewhat similar but more rapid with complex phrases.

Seasonal Abundance: Uncommon resident in Region, mid-April to October. Ranges in West from British Columbia to California, winters Mexico.

Where to Find: Low to mid-elevation mixed forests, oak woodlands. Migrants widespread anywhere with trees, including urban parks, neighborhoods. Best bets Larch Mountain (Columbia Gorge), Finley National Wildlife Refuge.

Habitat: Mixed, coniferous forests. Migrants use woodland edge, parks, neighborhoods.

Diet and Behavior: Forages sluggishly, deliberately in upper canopy for insects, some small fruits. Inconspicuous unless singing; may sing less frequently than other vireos. Joins mixed flocks in migration.

Voice: Song loud, consisting of simple, slurred, burry whistles with pauses between notes tending to be longer than notes. Calls include series of harsh, falling *shep* notes.

Did you know? Cassin's Vireo is the westernmost of three closely related species long classified as a single species, the Solitary Vireo. The other two are Plumbeous Vireo of the interior West and Blue-headed Vireo of the East.

Date and Location Seen: _____

Description: 4¾". Small, compact, **greenish-gray** above, lighter below with **white wing-bars**. Prominent, **diffuse white eye-ring** broken above eye, extending forward to thick, stubby bill. **Feet bluish-gray**.

Similar Species: Ruby-crowned Kinglet (page 277) almost identical, smaller with thin bill, yellowish feet, black below lower wing-bar. Tends to flick wings more often. Male kinglet's red crown may be hidden. Cassin's Vireo (page 223) larger with longer bill, well-defined spectacled appearance.

Seasonal Abundance: Fairly common but often overlooked resident in Region. Ranges from southwestern British Columbia down coast to California, also mountains from southeastern Arizona, southwestern Texas to Central America.

Where to Find: Lowlands to moderate elevations in foothills. Inconspicuous if not vocalizing. Typical sites: Mount Tabor Park (Portland), Skinner Butte (Eugene).

Habitat: Mixed woodlands, forest edge, thickets.

Diet and Behavior: Forages deliberately, mostly for insects, but takes some berries. Found often in pairs. Males sing constantly during brief period late winter–early spring. Joins mixed-species foraging flocks outside nesting season.

Voice: Song simple, slurred, whistled phrase repeated monotonously. Varied calls include rising *bree dee dee*, harsh mewing.

Did you know? Most vireos live in the tropics or migrate there for the winter. Hutton's is the only vireo to remain year round so far north.

Date and Location Seen: _____

Description: 5¼". More compact than warblers. **Plain grayish-green above**, whitish below. **Prominent light eyebrow** only distinguishing mark. Sometimes erects crest in excitement. JUVENILE: Yellower below.

Similar Species: Red-eyed Vireo (page 229) larger with longer bill, gray cap, eyebrow bordered with black above, below. Other vireos have wing-bars. Warblers yellower, thinner-billed.

Seasonal Abundance: Common resident in Region, May–September. Breeds from extreme southeastern Alaska to Maine, south in mountains to central Mexico; winters Mexico to northern Central America.

Where to Find: Widespread breeder from sea level to mountain passes except uncommon in urban areas. Common migrant throughout Region.

Habitat: Breeds in mixed open woodland, forest edge, aspen groves. Also found in mostly coniferous woods, but utilizes available broadleaf trees for nesting.

Diet and Behavior: Forages mostly in deciduous growth, primarily for insects; also some berries. Joins mixed flocks in migration. Sings often, even in migration, but difficult to spot due to slow foraging style.

Voice: Song extended, languid, rambling warble, different from other vireos — reminiscent of Purple Finch (page 359). Calls include nasal mewing.

Did you know? Vireos weave cup-shaped nests suspended from horizontal forked branches, sometimes placed at fairly low height.

Date and Location Seen: _____

Description: 5¾". Compact, short-tailed. Large, flat-looking head with heavy black bill. **Plain greenish above** except for **gray cap**; whitish below. **White eyebrow bordered with black line above, another below** passing through red eye. Sometimes erects crest in excitement. JUVENILE: Brown eye.

Similar Species: Warbling Vireo (page 227) smaller with shorter bill, lacks gray cap, black lines bordering eyebrow. Other vireos have wing-bars; warblers smaller.

Seasonal Abundance: Fairly common but local resident in Region, late May–August. North American population breeds across Canada, Northwest, East, winters in Amazon Basin. Other races resident in South America.

Where to Find: Nests mostly in major river valleys; rare migrant away from breeding sites. Best locations Sandy River below Sandy, Middle Fork Willamette River below Dexter.

Habitat: Prefers mature broadleaf woods, especially cottonwood groves along rivers. Also forests, parks with mature maple groves.

Diet and Behavior: Forages mostly in canopy, primarily on insects, but also eats berries (especially in fall). Sings persistently, but difficult to spot due to slow foraging style.

Voice: Song continuous, short but complex; low, whistled phrases given every couple of seconds. Calls include mewed *nyeeah*.

Did you know? Red-eyed Vireos have been observed singing while sitting on their nests.

Date and Location Seen: _____

Description: 12″. Medium-sized, **mostly blue**, long-tailed; upper body blackish with **long, prominent crest**, black banding on tail, wings. Sturdy blackish bill.

Similar Species: Western Scrub-Jay (page 233) without crest, blue above with brown back patch, white below, appears longer-tailed. Blue Jay (not shown; rare in Region) whitish below with broad white wing-bar.

Seasonal Abundance: Fairly common resident in Region. Ranges in West from south-central Alaska to Central American highlands.

Where to Find: Throughout Region to tree line.

Habitat: Coniferous, mixed forests, including forested urban areas. Exploits more open habitat in migration, winter.

Diet and Behavior: Omnivorous. Eats more seeds in fall, winter, frequents bird feeders. Garrulous, gregarious, forages mostly in trees but also to ground. Becomes secretive around bulky stick nest during spring. Some move southward or to lower elevations in winter.

Voice: Noisy, often heard before seen, with wide repertoire of calls; most common harsh *shaark shaark shraak*, also rapid *wek wek wek wek wek*.

Did you know? Although Steller's Jay is one of the commonest birds in Oregon, much remains to be learned about its habitat preferences and complex social system.

Date and Location Seen: _____

Description: 12". Medium-sized, long-tailed, **without crest. Blue above** with brown back patch, white eyebrow, dark cheek; **white below** with partial blue breast band.

Similar Species: Steller's Jay has prominent crest, upper body blackish, black banding on tail, wings. Blue Jay (not shown; rare in Region) crested, whitish below with broad white wing-bar.

Seasonal Abundance: Common resident in Region; continues to increase outside core valley areas. Ranges from Washington to Colorado, Texas, south to Mexican highlands.

Where to Find: Widespread in lowlands including cities, less so in foothills.

Habitat: Prefers deciduous, scrubby, open or semi-open terrain with thick brush; neighborhoods, gardens, farms, often near oaks.

Diet and Behavior: Omnivorous. Eats more seeds in fall, winter, often buries acorns for future retrieval, visits bird feeders. Forages frequently on ground, in brush, usually in flocks. Secretive when nesting.

Voice: Noisy with variety of calls; harsh, high-pitched, rising *sheeeenk* most often heard.

Did you know? Resident scrub-jay populations have extended their range northward from the southern Willamette Valley over the last century, thanks to their adaptability to human-wrought habitats. Scattered pairs are now found north to Seattle. Seventy-five years ago the same could be said for Portland, where the species flourishes today.

Date and Location Seen: _____

Description: 16". Chunky, but shape can vary in flight. **Completely black** with stout bill, **short, square, fan-shaped tail**. JUVENILE: Brownish-black with red mouth lining.

Similar Species: Common Raven (page 237) larger with wedge-shaped tail, longer bill, different voice; soars more, with wings held flat.

Seasonal Abundance: Common resident in Region. Ranges across North America from central Canada to southern U.S.

Where to Find: Abundant in cities, towns, agricultural areas, river valleys; less common in more-remote areas of dense coniferous forest, high mountains.

Habitat: Open woodlands, fields, clearings, cities, wherever trees available for nesting.

Diet and Behavior: Intelligent, highly gregarious. Omnivorous, opportunistic; feeds on refuse, handouts, road kills, crops, fruit, seeds, insects; raids other birds' nests for eggs, fledglings. Harasses predators noisily until they vacate crow territory or remain motionless in cover.

Voice: Noisy, garrulous. Common call *caww*.

Did you know? American Crows fly in large, noisy flocks in the evening toward roost sites in isolated stands of trees, often many miles from foraging areas.

Date and Location Seen: _____

COMMON RAVEN
Corvus corax

Description: 24". **Largest songbird**, with wingspan over four feet. **Entirely glossy-black** with long wings, **long, wedge-shaped tail, long, heavy, formidable bill**. Puffy throat, head feathers erected in display impart even larger look.

Similar Species: American Crow (page 235) smaller with shorter bill, different voice; lacks wedge-shaped tail. Ravens soar more often.

Seasonal Abundance: Fairly common resident in Region away from urban areas. Ranges across northern hemisphere from Arctic to temperate zone, south in mountains to Central America.

Where to Find: Nests middle to high elevations, widespread in winter away from cities.

Habitat: Coniferous, mixed forests; agricultural areas.

Diet and Behavior: Omnivorous, feeding on whatever available. Specializes in scavenging on large carcasses, descending on road kills, but also kills rodents, robs nests, feeds on insects. Highly intelligent, cautious; follows predators, hunters to take advantage of easy meal. Carries, hides food for future needs. Pairs, groups cavort in aerial displays.

Voice: Varied calls include harsh croak, liquid bell-like sounds, screamed *kraaah*, metallic rattles.

Did you know? Crows and ravens are always at odds. Ravens raid crow nests. Crows often swoop down on ravens while attempting to chase them away.

Date and Location Seen: _____

Alpine-breeding

Lowland-breeding

Description: 7¼". Grayish-brown above, white or yellow below with **black breast band**, white-edged dark tail. **Black mask, white or yellow eyebrow**; small, dark "horns" protrude from crown behind eye. FEMALE: Paler, horns inconspicuous.

Similar Species: Combination of breast band, mask, horns distinctive. Other open-country songbirds with white outer tails: American Pipit (page 293) pumps tail constantly; Vesper Sparrow (page 325) with strongly streaked back, heavier bill, white eye-ring; Western Meadowlark (page 349) larger.

Seasonal Abundance: Locally common resident in Region. Nests throughout North America, Mexico; also Eurasia, North Africa. Northern, alpine populations migrate south or to lowlands in winter.

Where to Find: Nests in alpine tundra in Cascades, open meadowlands in Willamette Valley. Large flocks winter throughout lowlands.

Habitat: Fields, short-grass meadows with patches of bare ground.

Diet and Behavior: Mainly insects in summer, seeds, grain in winter. Forages on bare ground or low vegetation.

Voice: Light, continuous *tsip tsip tsee di di*, usually given from fence line or other elevated perch, often in flight display overhead.

Did you know? Known as Shore Lark in the Old World, the Horned Lark is a widespread, variable species. In the Willamette Valley Region, the lowland-breeding race is more colorful and strongly patterned than alpine-breeding birds.

Date and Location Seen: _____

Male

Female

Description: 8". **Large**, long-winged swallow with **shallowly forked tail**, relatively large bill. MALE: Adult **entirely dark-purplish-blue**. First-year male resembles female with some blue below. FEMALE: **Gray of throat, chest extends around neck** in collar; belly dingy-whitish; back, tail, face all-dark.

Similar Species: Larger than other swallows, soars more. European Starling (page 291) stubby with shorter tail.

Seasonal Abundance: Uncommon to locally fairly common resident in Region, mid-April to September. Ranges throughout eastern North America west to prairie provinces, West Coast south from British Columbia; also locally in interior West. Winters in South America.

Where to Find: Conspicuous at nesting sites, e.g., Sauvie Island, Fern Ridge Reservoir. Seldom seen foraging elsewhere or in migration.

Habitat: Open areas, mostly near water.

Diet and Behavior: Forages in flight for insects. Flocks in migration, sometimes with other swallows. Nests in small colonies, mostly in boxes, gourds provided by humans. Competes with other cavity nesters; sharply declined with European Starling introduction, but martins succeed in nest sites over water, often on pilings.

Voice: Song low-pitched, liquid warbles. Calls include rich, descending *cher cher*, rattle in alarm.

Did you know? Eastern Purple Martin populations are highly colonial, using multi-unit nest structures. Western populations are only loosely colonial, shunning multi-unit boxes.

Date and Location Seen: _____

Male

Female First-year

Description: 5¾". Relatively stocky. Broad, triangular wings; short, slightly notched tail. **Glossy, iridescent-blue above, bright-white underparts**. FEMALE: Duller, with brown upperparts in first year changing to blue with age. JUVENILE: Plain brown above.

Similar Species: Violet-green Swallow (page 245) greener with white "saddlebag" flank patches, white cheek extending above eye. Juveniles difficult to separate. Northern Rough-winged Swallow (page 247) has dusky throat, upper breast.

Seasonal Abundance: Common summer resident in Region, arrives by February, begins to depart by July, most gone before September. Rare in winter. Breeds from Alaska to Labrador south through most of U.S., winters southern U.S., West Indies, Mexico, Central America.

Where to Find: Widespread but local at mostly low or moderate elevation, usually near water.

Habitat: Open areas near water with trees, boxes for nest sites.

Diet and Behavior: Forages in flight for insects. Eats some berries during migration, winter. Forms large flocks in migration, sometimes with other swallows. Nests in pairs but also in loose colonies, using natural cavities, nest boxes. Competes with other species for nest sites.

Voice: Song composed of series of chirps, warbles. Calls include liquid *chweet*, chattering in alarm.

Did you know? The Tree Swallow is the only songbird species in which one-year-old females have a different, distinct immature plumage.

Date and Location Seen: _____

Male

VIOLET-GREEN SWALLOW
Tachycineta thalassina

Description: 5¼". Fairly **petite**, long-winged, with slightly notched tail. **White below**, including **saddlebag-like flank patches**. MALE: Glossy, iridescent-purple-green above with **white extending above eye**. FEMALE: Duller; bronze-green with gray wash below, duskier cheek. JUVENILE: Lacks green.

Similar Species: Tree Swallow (page 243) bluer, with dark cheek, flanks.

Seasonal Abundance: Common summer resident in Region, begins to return by late February, departs by October. Breeds in West from Alaska to Mexico; winters Mexico, northern Central America.

Where to Find: Widespread, from lowlands up to fairly high elevations.

Habitat: Open areas including woodlands, cities, agricultural lands; often near water in migration.

Diet and Behavior: Forages in flight for insects, often at great height. Forms large flocks in migration, sometimes with other swallows. Nests in pairs but may be found in small colonies, nesting in cliff crevices, under building eaves, or in natural cavities, nest boxes. Scouts openings in buildings for potential nest sites.

Voice: Song repeated *tsip tseet tsip*, reminiscent of Pine Siskin. Calls include *chilip* — higher, sharper than Tree Swallow.

Did you know? Male Violet-green Swallows sing their courtship song monotonously in the pre-dawn darkness.

Date and Location Seen: _____

Description: 5¾". Bulkier than most swallows, with smooth, deep wing-beats, square tail. **Plain brownish above**, whitish below, with **dingy-gray throat, upper breast**. JUVENILE: Cinnamon on wings.

Similar Species: Cliff Swallow (page 249) has rusty-orange rump, white forehead spot. Female Purple Martin (page 241) larger, tail forked. Bank Swallow (not shown; rare in Region) smaller with white throat, distinct brown breast band. Other white-bellied swallows have white throats.

Seasonal Abundance: Fairly common resident in Region, mid-March–September. Breeds across North America from southern Alaska to Maritimes, south through Central America; northern populations move south in winter.

Where to Find: Throughout Region, mostly at lower elevations.

Habitat: Open areas, usually near water, especially cut streambanks.

Diet and Behavior: Forages in flight low over water, fields, for insects. Less likely to flock than other swallows, but joins mixed groups of swallows. Not colonial nester, but favorable site may attract more than one pair. Uses old burrow nests of other species, culvert pipe, other tubular man-made structures. Sometimes digs nest burrow.

Voice: Song rough, repeated *frrep*. Call harsh, low *breet*.

Did you know? The "rough-winged" moniker comes from the small serrations this species shows on its wing feathers.

Date and Location Seen: _____

Description: 5½". Compact swallow with **square, dark tail, rusty-buff rump. Dark-chestnut throat, cheek** contrast with whitish underparts. **Light forehead spot**, buff collar stand out from dark cap, dark back streaked with white. Long, dark, pointed wings, tiny feet, bill.

Similar Species: Other swallows lack orange-buff rump.

Seasonal Abundance: Common resident in Region, mid-March–September. Breeds across North America from Arctic to Mexico, winters in South America.

Where to Find: Widespread in open lowlands, ranging up some river drainages into mountains.

Habitat: Open areas, often near water; nests on cliffs or man-made structures, preferably of concrete, such as bridges, dams, buildings.

Diet and Behavior: Forages in flight for insects. Flocks at all seasons, nests in colonies. Each pair builds gourd-shaped nest on vertical surface with some overhead protection, using mud pellets. Enters nest through short, narrow tunnel. Stages in large numbers away from nest sites when young fledge, then departs for South America.

Voice: Song thin, harsh twitters, given in series. Calls include husky *churr*, soft, low *veew* given in alarm.

Did you know? Other birds use Cliff Swallow nests for roosting in winter.

Date and Location Seen: _____

Description: 7". **Streamlined**, graceful in flight. Blue-black above, **long, forked tail** with white spot near tip of each tail feather. Long, dark, pointed wings. **Cinnamon-buff below** with **dark breast band**, rusty throat, forehead, small black bill. Perches upright with tiny feet. JUVENILE: Pale beneath; without tail streamers.

Similar Species: Other swallows lack forked tail. Purple Martin (page 241) larger, tail much less forked.

Seasonal Abundance: Common resident in Region, mid-March–September; migrants continue through October. Rare in winter. Breeds around northern hemisphere from Arctic to subtropical zone; winters to southern hemisphere, mostly in tropics.

Where to Find: Throughout Region; most common near man-made structures.

Habitat: Open habitats with buildings, bridges, culverts for nesting. Tends to be near water in migration.

Diet and Behavior: Forages in flight for insects. Flocks in migration, often with other swallows. Builds nest from mud, grasses, lined with feathers, often inside or beneath structures, choosing mostly horizontal but also vertical surfaces.

Voice: Song string of squeaky, twittering notes, grating sounds. Calls include *vit*, emphatic *pit veet* given in alarm.

Did you know? The Barn Swallow has adapted nearly completely to nesting on man-made structures. Nests built on natural sites such as shallow caves and crevices are rarely found.

Date and Location Seen: _____

Description: 5¼". Typical chickadee, with **white cheek dividing dark cap from black bib**. Small, thin bill. **Cap black**, belly white, sides buffy, wings, tail, **back gray**. Willamette Valley populations duskier than birds east of Cascades.

Similar Species: Chestnut-backed Chickadee (page 255) smaller with sooty-brown cap, chestnut sides, back. Mountain Chickadee (page 379) has white eyebrow.

Seasonal Abundance: Common resident in Region. Ranges from Alaska to Newfoundland, south to New Mexico, Tennessee.

Where to Find: Throughout Region although absent from higher elevations; most common wooded lowland stream-banks.

Habitat: Broadleaf, mixed woods, thickets, neighborhoods. Prefers deciduous growth, especially alders.

Diet and Behavior: Searches for insects, seeds among branches, hanging upside down to glean leaf undersides. Highly sociable when not nesting — forms small flocks, joins mixed flocks. Uses cavities, nest boxes, sometimes in backyards. Visits bird feeders, storing seeds in tree bark nearby.

Voice: Song clear, whistled *fee bee*, less often 3–5 note *fee fee fee*. Calls include familiar *chick a dee dee dee*.

Did you know? Chickadees are capable of going into a night torpor, which saves energy.

Date and Location Seen: _____

CHESTNUT-BACKED CHICKADEE
Poecile rufescens

Description: 4¾". Typical chickadee with **white cheek dividing dark cap from black bib. Cap sooty-brown; sides, back rich-chestnut**; small, thin bill, grayish wings, tail.

Similar Species: Black-capped Chickadee (page 253) slightly larger with black cap, lacks chestnut color. Mountain Chickadee (page 379) with white eyebrow, also lacks chestnut.

Seasonal Abundance: Common resident in Region. Ranges from south-central Alaska to central California, mostly along coast, but inland across Washington, southern British Columbia to northwestern Montana.

Where to Find: Throughout Region from just below tree line to lowlands, including cities.

Habitat: Coniferous forest; also mixed woods, but seldom far from conifers. Dispersing birds in fall may use deciduous woodlands.

Diet and Behavior: Forages among branches for insects, seeds, some berries, hanging upside down while gleaning on twigs. May form larger flocks than Black-capped; flocks with it, other species. Uses cavities, nest boxes, sometimes in backyards. Visits bird feeders, often storing seeds in tree bark nearby.

Voice: *Chick zee zee* call higher, hoarser than other chickadees in Region. Lacks whistled song of Black-capped.

Did you know? When they must excavate their own nest cavities Chestnut-backeds and other chickadees often choose decaying snags, in deference to their tiny bills.

Date and Location Seen: _____

Male

Female

Description: 4″. **Tiny, plain** grayish, **nondescript** but lighter underneath, browner on head with **long tail**. Bill tiny, blackish, slightly downcurved. Eye white in female, dark in male, juvenile.

Similar Species: Chickadees have white cheek patches. Kinglets have wing-bars, shorter tails.

Seasonal Abundance: Common resident in Region at lower elevations. Ranges in West from southwestern British Columbia to Guatemala.

Where to Find: Throughout lowlands, following some river drainages into mountains; numerous in urban areas.

Habitat: Broadleaf, mixed woodlands, open forest, parks, neighborhoods.

Diet and Behavior: Forages in flocks except during short period while nesting. Groups of up to fifty individuals move from tree to tree in tight line, almost in single file. Feeds mostly on insects but may eat seeds, berries. Visits suet feeders. Builds extraordinary hanging nest woven of moss, lichen, spider web, other materials, up to a foot long with small entrance near top, usually less than ten feet from ground.

Voice: Calls given by flocking birds include short *tsip*, trilled alarm call.

Did you know? Bushtits are the smallest North American birds by weight except for the hummingbirds.

Date and Location Seen: _____

Description: 4¼". **Stubby-tailed**, with straight, chisel-like bill. Gray above, **rusty underneath, white eyebrow** separates black cap from **black eye-line**. MALE: Brighter than female, juvenile.

Similar Species: White-breasted Nuthatch (page 261) larger with plain white face, rust limited to undertail. Among other bark-clinging birds, Brown Creeper (page 263) streaked above, woodpeckers much larger. Chickadees have longer tails, white cheek patch.

Seasonal Abundance: Common resident in Region. Numbers variably increase in lowland urban areas due to migration, downslope movement in winter. Breeds in conifer-forest zones across Canada, northern, western U.S. Winters south to Florida, Texas some years.

Where to Find: Throughout Region from tree line to lowlands, including urban areas.

Habitat: Coniferous, mixed forests, parks, woodlots.

Diet and Behavior: Acrobatically climbs up, down tree trunks in search of insect prey, mostly in summer. More dependent on seeds in winter, particularly from conifers; may migrate from areas without adequate cone crop. Excavates nest cavity in rotten wood. Joins mixed-species flocks outside nesting season. Regular at sunflower, suet bird feeders.

Voice: Calls include short nasal *enk* given in series.

Did you know? Red-breasted Nuthatches smear conifer sap around their nest holes to deter predators.

Date and Location Seen: _____

Description: 5¾". **Stubby-tailed**, with thin, straight, needle-like bill. Gray above; black cap, nape; **white face, underparts**; rusty undertail. **Clings to bark**, walking up, down limbs, trunks. MALE: Cap, nape blacker than female, juvenile.

Similar Species: Red-breasted Nuthatch (page 259) entirely rusty below with prominent black eye-line. Brown Creeper (page 263) streaked above. Woodpeckers larger.

Seasonal Abundance: Fairly common but local resident in Region; declining in north with loss of preferred habitat. Ranges across North America from Canada to Mexican highlands.

Where to Find: Mainly in oak woodlands, e.g., Sauvie Island, Finley National Wildlife Refuge. Nearly extirpated in western Washington.

Habitat: Strongly linked to oak groves (especially older stands), also uses mixed woodlands; avoids dense conifers.

Diet and Behavior: Explores large limbs for insect prey; in winter, eats more seeds, forages on smaller branches, attracted to sunflower, suet feeders. Uses natural cavity, old woodpecker hole, occasionally provided box for nesting.

Voice: Calls include harsh nasal yelps; more-complex courtship calls in spring include series of clear whistles.

Did you know? White-breasted Nuthatches west of the Cascades belong to a distinct coastal subspecies known as Slender-billed Nuthatch, now threatened due to the slow dying out of their oak habitat.

Date and Location Seen: _____

Description: 5¼″. Slim, **streaked brownish-gray above** except for plain rusty rump, **white eyebrow**; white below, brightest on chin, breast. **Hitches up tree trunks** with long, stiff tail. Bill long, thin, downcurved.

Similar Species: Red-breasted Nuthatch (page 259) unstreaked, reddish below. Woodpeckers much larger. Bewick's Wren (page 265) sometimes goes up trees; has more-uniform brown upperparts, longer, free-wheeling tail.

Seasonal Abundance: Fairly common resident throughout Region. Some downslope movement occurs in winter. Breeds in forest zones from Alaska to Labrador, Middle Atlantic states, south through western U.S. to Central America. Some winter across rest of continent to northeastern Mexico.

Where to Find: Throughout Region to mountain passes, including urban areas.

Habitat: Forests, open groves, parks containing good-sized trees.

Diet and Behavior: Forages for insects while hitching up bark of tree using tail as brace. Probes crevices as it climbs, then flies down low onto next tree, begins again. Builds nest under sheets of loose bark on trunks, large branches. Joins mixed-species flocks outside nesting season.

Voice: Song high-pitched rising, falling notes in series, often ending on high note. Call high, thin *tseee*.

Did you know? The sight of the Brown Creeper's white breast as it moves up the tree may cause prey to move, facilitating detection.

Date and Location Seen: _____

Description: 5¼". Slim, **plain brown**, with **bold white eyebrow**, long, thin downcurved bill, **long, brown tail** with fine dark bands above, **black-and-white edging, undersurface**. Often flicks tail from side to side.

Similar Species: House Wren (page 267), Marsh Wren (page 271) with much fainter eyebrows. Winter Wren (page 269) tiny, darker, with stubby tail.

Seasonal Abundance: Common resident in Region. Ranges from southwestern British Columbia to California, across southwestern states to Texas, Mexico; spottily distributed east of Mississippi River.

Where to Find: Widespread in lowlands, including cities. Frequent in backyards.

Habitat: Forest edge, open habitats at lower elevations including hedgerows, thickets, areas near human habitation.

Diet and Behavior: Forages mostly for insects, some berries in dense undergrowth, but also probes bark on larger limbs, feeds on ground. Nests in thickets or cavities, often in man-made objects.

Voice: Song extremely variable, loud series of warbles, ringing trills, beginning with soft buzz that sounds like inhalation; easily confused with Song Sparrow (page 331). Calls numerous, including scolding, harsh notes, sharp *jik*.

Did you know? Bewick's Wren was once more common and widespread in eastern North America than in the West. For unknown reasons the situation has reversed in recent decades, as eastern populations continue to decline sharply while western populations expand.

Date and Location Seen: _____

Description: 4¾". Nondescript. **Plain brown, paler below**, with **thin bill**. Fine, dark banding on wings, tail; vague line through eye. **Light eye-ring**. Often holds tail at upward angle.

Similar Species: Bewick's Wren (page 265) larger, with bold white eyebrow. Winter Wren (page 269) darker, with short tail. Marsh Wren (page 271) in wet habitat, with whitish eyebrow, streaks on back; plain juveniles difficult to separate.

Seasonal Abundance: Fairly common summer resident in Region, April–September. Northern form, often considered separate species, breeds across southern Canada, most of U.S., winters southern U.S., Mexico. Other forms resident Mexico to South America.

Where to Find: Widespread, mostly lowland woodlots, streamside vegetation.

Habitat: Drier forest edge, semi-open habitats at lower elevations including clearcuts, areas near human habitation.

Diet and Behavior: Forages on ground, bushes for insects. Nests in cavities, including nest boxes. Competes for nest sites with other species. Males vigorously protect territory with constant singing.

Voice: Song exuberant, bubbling trills, whistled notes, given in rapid series. Calls include scolding, rattling, nasal mewing.

Did you know? The male House Wren fills many prospective nest holes with materials and the female lays eggs in one.

Date and Location Seen: _____

Description: 4″. **Tiny, round, with stubby tail**, thin bill, light-brown eyebrow. Chocolate-brown above, **fine, dark banding on tail, wings, belly. Breast rich-rufous-brown**. Secretive but constantly active.

Similar Species: Bewick's Wren (page 265) larger, with bold white eyebrow. House Wren (page 267) with light breast, longer tail. Marsh Wren (page 271) with whitish eyebrow, streaked back.

Seasonal Abundance: Common resident in Region. Breeds in conifer-forest zones of Alaska, Canada, northern U.S., south in mountains, along West Coast; winters milder parts of breeding range, Midwest, Southeast. Also resident in Eurasia.

Where to Find: Throughout Region. Breeds to mountain passes, withdraws to below level of heavy snow in winter. Frequent then in neighborhoods, parks, but tends to breed away from urbanization.

Habitat: Nests in wet underbrush of coniferous forest. Dense forest, thickets, tangles in winter, migration.

Diet and Behavior: Moves mouse-like through low undergrowth, eating insects; may also eat berries. Investigates intruders from open perch while bobbing up-and-down. Males sing from low, hidden or mid-level, exposed perches.

Voice: Song remarkable lengthy series of varied tinkling trills, warbles. Calls include oft-given *chit chit*, rapid, staccato series of chips.

Did you know? Curiosity sometimes brings Winter Wrens inside buildings where they can become trapped.

Date and Location Seen: _____

MARSH WREN
Cistothorus palustris

Description: 4¾". **Secretive** but curious. Brown above with **fine dark banding on wings, tail**, plain grayish below; **tail held cocked up. Dark cap, white eyebrow, faint white streaks on upper back**. Long, thin bill curves down. JUVENILE: Appears almost plain brown with vague light eyebrow.

Similar Species: House Wren (page 267) plainer with only very faint eyebrow. Bewick's Wren (page 265) larger, with bolder white eyebrow. Winter Wren (page 269) darker, with short tail.

Seasonal Abundance: Common resident in Region, less so in winter. Breeds across continent from British Columbia to New England, south to California, Gulf Coast (but absent in interior Southeast); winters south to Mexico.

Where to Find: Widespread throughout Region at lower elevations, in appropriate habitat.

Habitat: Marshes with thick emergent vegetation, usually cattails; also river edge, wet fields, scrub adjacent to wetlands.

Diet and Behavior: Forages low, crawling within thick cover, mostly for insects. Male sings day or night from exposed or hidden perches with tail cocked, often flat against back.

Voice: Song mechanical but musical rattled trill begun with a few call notes. Call distinctive *tik*.

Did you know? The male Marsh Wren builds multiple spherical nests amidst emergent stalks; the female chooses one to line and lay eggs in.

Date and Location Seen: _____

Description: 7½". Stout, **chunky, uniform slate-gray**, with **short tail**, thin, straight bill, pale legs. Shape, **bobbing motions** suggest large wren. Often flashes white eyelids. JUVENILE: Spotted breast.

Similar Species: Distinctive; much larger than any wren in Region.

Seasonal Abundance: Uncommon resident in Region, mostly mountains, foothills in summer; may be seen in more-urbanized areas in winter. Ranges in western mountains from Aleutians to Central America.

Where to Find: During nesting season, rushing streams (less frequently ponds) from middle elevations up to tree line. Moves downstream in winter to larger rivers, suburban creeks. Good bet Multnomah Falls, other Columbia Gorge streams.

Habitat: Rushing streams, rivers, pond margins. Occasional at stream mouths in winter.

Diet and Behavior: Swims or walks on stream bottoms in pursuit of aquatic insect larvae, mollusks, small fish, fish eggs. Stands, bobs on streamside rocks, flying up, down stream to feed, protect territory. Builds bulky, domed nest next to streams, often under bridges. Uses wings to "fly" underwater.

Voice: Song loud, piercing musical whistles repeated in series. Calls include buzzy *bzzeet*.

Did you know? Dippers are the only true aquatic songbirds.

Date and Location Seen: _____

GOLDEN-CROWNED KINGLET
Regulus satrapa

Description: 3¾". **Tiny**, with **short, notched tail**, thin bill, constant, **nervous wing-flitting**. Olive-gray above, grayish-white below, **white wing-bars, dark flight feathers with golden edging**. Broad **white eyebrow below black-striped crown**, crown center orange-and-yellow in male, yellow in female; colors may be obscured.

Similar Species: Ruby-crowned Kinglet (page 277) slightly larger, greener; has eye-ring, no head stripes. Warblers larger.

Seasonal Abundance: Common resident in Region. Breeds in conifer-forest zones from southeastern Alaska across continent to Newfoundland, south in mountains to Guatemala; winters through all but northernmost parts of breeding range south across U.S. to northeastern Mexico.

Where to Find: Throughout Region including lowlands, mountains, cities.

Habitat: Breeds in conifer stands, winters in mixed woods; migrants appear anywhere.

Diet and Behavior: Forages high, low, although when nesting tends to remain high. Gregarious when not nesting. Prefers conifers but seeks out insects in low deciduous growth, climbing, gleaning, hanging upside down, moving rapidly in flocks. Joins mixed flocks.

Voice: Song begins with three high, thin notes, ends with tumbling chatter. Call thin *tsee tsee tsee* or *tsee*.

Did you know? The English and Latin names of kinglets reflect the jeweled crowns and assertive behavior of these "little kings".

Date and Location Seen: _____

RUBY-CROWNED KINGLET
Regulus calendula

Description: 4". **Tiny, plump-appearing, with short tail**, thin bill, constant, **nervous wing-flitting**. Greenish-gray above, lighter below. **Dark wings with white wing-bars**, blackish below lower bar. Prominent but diffuse **white eye-ring**. Red crown of male usually obscured.

Similar Species: Golden-crowned Kinglet (page 275) has light eyebrow below black stripe, no eye-ring. Hutton's Vireo (page 225) very similar but larger with thicker bill, blue-gray not yellowish feet; lacks black below lower wing-bar.

Seasonal Abundance: Common migrant, winter resident in lowlands of Region, September to early May. Nests sparingly high in Cascades, on fringe of Region. Breeding range from Alaska, British Columbia to Labrador, south in mountains of West; winters Pacific Coast, southern states to Guatemala.

Where to Find: Winters throughout lowlands in urban, agricultural settings, remote areas. Up to mountain passes in migration.

Habitat: Breeds in coniferous forest; prefers thickets, brush, forest edge in winter.

Diet and Behavior: Forages low or high, mostly for insects. Eats some berries. Congregates in attractive habitats. Joins mixed-species flocks.

Voice: Song long, rolling series of trills, twitters, repeated phrases, often heard in spring migration. Call low, husky *jidit*.

Did you know? Curious and easily attracted, male Ruby-crowned Kinglets display their red crowns aggressively when agitated.

Date and Location Seen: _____

Male

Female

Description: 6¾". Small, **upright thrush** with short, thin bill, **solid blue wings, tail**. MALE: Bright-blue above with **rusty-brown breast**, gray belly. FEMALE: Less blue; back, head grayish, breast pale-rust. JUVENILE: Grayer with vague speckling, **whitish eye-ring**.

Similar Species: Mountain Bluebird (page 381) usually lacks rusty tones on breast. Male Lazuli Bunting (page 345) smaller with white wing-bars, finch-like bill.

Seasonal Abundance: Uncommon resident in Region. Ranges from British Columbia to highlands of Mexico; northern populations move south in winter.

Where to Find: Foothills, mainly where bluebird nest-box "trails" established; mostly lowlands in winter.

Habitat: Meadows, clearcuts with standing snags, farms, open woods.

Diet and Behavior: Forages mostly on insects, also berries, especially after summer. Hunts from low perch over short grass, may hover before capture. Flocks outside nesting season. Cavity nester; readily accepts nest boxes mounted at open sites near ground.

Voice: Seldom sings. Calls include low, chattering, whistled *chwer*.

Did you know? For decades, Western Bluebirds seriously declined in the Willamette Valley Region from loss of nest cavities. Numbers have increased greatly in recent years due to aggressive nest-box campaigns.

Date and Location Seen: _____

Description: 7″. **Plain warm-brown above** from head to tail. Buff breast with small dark spots. Thin bill, brown face with diffuse, **buffy eye-ring** extending to bill, giving spectacled appearance.

Similar Species: Hermit Thrush (page 283) with contrasting rusty tail, thin white eye-ring, habit of cocking tail. Juvenile American Robin (page 285) much larger, some orange on breast.

Seasonal Abundance: Common migrant, summer resident throughout Region, May–October. Breeds from Alaska across Canada, northern states to Newfoundland, south to California in West. Winters from Mexico to South America.

Where to Find: Throughout Region. Mostly breeds away from urbanized areas. Migrants secretive but widespread.

Habitat: Leafy deciduous or mixed woods, often near streams. Prefers dense understory cover with salmonberry, other native shrubs.

Diet and Behavior: Forages on ground but also often in trees, unlike Hermit Thrush. Feeds on insects, berries. Retiring; most often identified by distinctive voice.

Voice: Song — series of nasal whistles spiraling upward — may be mistaken for that of Purple Finch (page 359). Calls include low, whistled *whit*.

Did you know? Swainson's Thrushes migrate at night and are regularly heard calling back and forth to each other as they pass overhead.

Date and Location Seen: _____

Description: 6¾". **Plain grayish-brown upperparts contrast with reddish-brown rump, tail**. Buffy-white breast with dark spots, gray flanks. Thin bill, **thin white eye-ring** on brown face. Head grayish or brownish dependent on race.

Similar Species: Swainson's Thrush (page 281) lacks reddish tail; rarely cocks tail. Fox Sparrow (page 329) with conical bill.

Seasonal Abundance: Fairly common summer resident, uncommon in winter, widespread migrant (mid-April–mid-May, September–October). Breeds across continent from Alaska to Newfoundland; winters coasts, southern U.S., south to Central America.

Where to Find: Breeds mostly at middle to high elevations in Cascades, rarely Coast Range; winters throughout lowlands.

Habitat: Coniferous, mixed forests, including older, regenerating clearcuts. In winter, thickets, forest edge, parks, neighborhoods.

Diet and Behavior: Forages mostly on ground, often in open woodlands, for insects, fruit; feeds on fruit in trees. Cocks, then slowly lowers tail while pumping wings, giving call note (unlike Swainson's Thrush). Sings from high perches in trees. Seldom flocks, but may feed in fruiting trees with other species.

Voice: Song consists of ethereal, spiraling whistles given at different pitches. Calls include rising *zhweeee*, muffled *chup*.

Did you know? Hermit Thrushes sometimes stir leaf litter with one foot to flush prey.

Date and Location Seen: _____

Male

Juvenile

Description: 10″. Bulky, with solid gray back. **Upright stance**. Thin but fairly stout yellow bill, dark stripes on white throat, **dull-orange breast**, white undertail, **white marks above, below eye**. MALE: Darker, head blackish. FEMALE: Breast lighter orange. JUVENILE: Spotted breast.

Similar Species: Other thrushes smaller without orange breast. Spotted Towhee (page 321) smaller with white belly.

Seasonal Abundance: Common resident in Region. Breeds across North America, south in mountains of Mexico; winters from southern part of breeding range south to Guatemala.

Where to Find: Ubiquitous. Backyards to mountains.

Habitat: Forests, cities, lawns, open areas. Nests wherever trees, structures present for nest placement, mud available for construction.

Diet and Behavior: Runs on ground or stands still while searching for insects, worms. Takes fruits from bushes, trees, ground. Winter flocks can number in thousands. Roosts communally at night in dense vegetation, often near fruit. May migrate if driven south by cold, but usually returns north as soon as temperature allows.

Voice: Song familiar lengthy, rich caroling, consisting of rising, falling phrases. Calls include *tuk tuk tuk*, sharp *piik* given in alarm, high, thin *sreep* in flight.

Did you know? The American Robin takes its name from an Old World flycatcher that is also orange-breasted, though not closely related.

Date and Location Seen: _____

Male

Female

Description: 9½". **Chunky, with short tail, dark breast band, dark mask**, bill. **Orange eyebrow**, breast, throat, wing patches, broad wing-bars. MALE: **Bluish-gray**, cap to tail; breast band, mask black. FEMALE: Brownish-gray mask, upperparts, with faint breast band.

Similar Species: American Robin (page 285) with longer tail, no breast band.

Seasonal Abundance: Common resident in Region, now breeds almost exclusively in mountains due to fragmentation of lowland forests. Fairly common in lowlands by October, leaves by April. Breeding range extends from Alaska, Yukon to northern California; vacates high mountains, northern parts of range in winter as birds move downslope or farther south (as far as southern California).

Where to Find: Throughout Region, mountains in summer, below level of heavy snow in winter, including neighborhoods, parks.

Habitat: Prefers moist coniferous forest, thick understory.

Diet and Behavior: Forages for insects, fruits in trees, on ground. Eats mostly fruit in winter, sometimes visits sunflower feeders; may congregate near madrone, ornamentals. Flocks less than robins, but gregarious at times in migration, winter. Male sings year-round from high perches.

Voice: Song fairly long, ethereal, trilled whistle, repeated at different pitches after long pauses. Calls include *chup* similar to Hermit Thrush (page 283).

Did you know? Varied Thrushes wander regularly as far as the East Coast.

Date and Location Seen: _____

Description: 6¼". **Plain**, brush-loving, grayish, with rounded **long tail often held cocked up; eye whitish, short bill** blackish, pinkish-brown breast obscurely streaked.

Similar Species: Bushtit (page 257) much smaller, usually in flocks; wrens have longer bills, dark eyes, shorter tails.

Seasonal Abundance: Uncommon resident, present only at southern, western edges of Region, but expanding, increasing. Ranges along coast, Oregon to northern Baja California.

Where to Find: Eastern slope of Coast Range and adjacent lowlands, also Cascade drainages north to Linn County. Despite recent range extensions, rare north of Yamhill County, has not reached Washington.

Habitat: Low, dense thickets, evergreen brush in open woodlands, shrubby regenerating clearcuts at higher elevations.

Diet and Behavior: Very secretive, seldom leaves thick brush; most often recognized by voice. Forages mainly on insects, fruits more in fall; may feed hanging upside down. Often found in pairs with both sexes singing year-round. Stays close to home, with limited fall dispersal into non-breeding areas.

Voice: Male "bouncing-ball" song a few clear whistles accelerating to descending trill; female *churrr*. Calls include grating *prr prr prr*.

Did you know? Unique in many ways, the Wrentit was long classified in a family of its own. Its closest affinities are with the babblers, an Old World family; its nearest relatives live in China.

Date and Location Seen: _____

Breeding

Non-breeding

Juvenile

Description: 8". Chunky, with **short tail, long, thin, pointed bill**. Short tail, gliding habit impart **triangular appearance in flight**. BREEDING: Plain, **iridescent-blackish** with minimal brown feather edging, **yellow bill**. NON-BREEDING: Heavy white spotting, prominent brown feather edging throughout; dark bill. JUVENILE: **Plain grayish-brown**, dark bill.

Similar Species: Western Meadowlark (page 349) with white outer tail feathers, yellow breast. Blackbirds with longer tails, more-conical bills.

Seasonal Abundance: Common year-round resident in Region. Original range Eurasia; introduced in many other parts of world including North America, where now found from Alaska, Labrador to West Indies, Mexico.

Where to Find: Throughout Region. Abundant in urban, agricultural areas, scarce in mountains, dense forest.

Habitat: Disturbed habitats including cities, parks, open woods, farms.

Diet and Behavior: Probes ground for insects. Forages in trees, on ground for whatever food available, often flycatches like swallows. Highly gregarious, gathering in noisy flocks of thousands, especially at evening roosts. May nest several times per year, competing for nest cavities with native species. Sings year round from prominent perches, sometimes while flapping wings like wind-up toy.

Voice: Continuous series of squeaks, squawks, including mimicry of other species.

Did you know? Introduced in New York in 1890, European Starlings expanded across the continent, reaching the Region in 1947.

Date and Location Seen: _____

Description: 6½". **Slender**, sparrow-like, with **long, dark, white-edged tail**, long, thin bill. Plain gray-brown above with faint wing-bars, variably **streaked below**, mostly on buff-white upper breast. Light eyebrow, eye-ring, mustache mark. **Bobs tail** while walking on ground to feed.

Similar Species: Thin bill, tail-bobbing separate pipits from sparrows.

Seasonal Abundance: Common migrant, local winter resident in lowlands of Region; summer resident above timberline in Cascades. Breeds across North America to eastern Siberia, south in mountains to New Mexico. Winters both coasts, southern interior states, Mexico.

Where to Find: High Cascades in summer, open agricultural fields in winter, mainly Linn, Benton Counties.

Habitat: Breeds in high-elevation tundra; migrants, winter birds use plowed fields, meadows, dried pond margins, shorelines.

Diet and Behavior: Usually walks on ground, foraging for seeds, insects. Flocks at all seasons except when nesting. Can be tame, approachable, but entire flock may flush if alarm call given.

Voice: Sharp distinctive *pi pit* call, given often in flight.

Did you know? American Pipits in breeding plumage are somewhat more lightly streaked beneath than in non-breeding plumage. Some breeding individuals may be completely unstreaked.

Date and Location Seen: _____

Juvenile

Description: 7¼". **Sleek, crested**. Silky-brown head, back grade into gray rump. Black mask, chin, **yellow belly, white undertail**. Plain gray wings with **waxy red spots**. Blackish, square, **short tail with yellow tip**. JUVENILE: Duller with streaks below.

Similar Species: Distinctive. European Starling (page 291) has same triangular, short-tailed shape in flight, but larger with different markings.

Seasonal Abundance: Common summer resident in Region, becomes rare most winters. Returns by mid-May, almost all have moved south by November. Largest flocks appear in fall, include many juveniles. Breeds across southern Canada, northern U.S., winters south to West Indies, Panama.

Where to Find: Throughout Region, including urban areas.

Habitat: Open forest, forest edge, city parks, neighborhoods near ornamental plantings.

Diet and Behavior: Eats mostly small fruits but often flycatches during summer. Tends to flock except when nesting, descends on ripe fruit en masse. Tight, swirling flocks can number in hundreds. Calls frequently in flight, while perched.

Voice: Call high-pitched, thin *sreeee*.

Did you know? Cedar Waxwings nest late to exploit the availability of ripe fruit.

Date and Location Seen: _____

Breeding form

Gray-headed form

Description: 4¾". **Plain** with obscure markings, faint, blurred breast streaks, no wing-bars, **small, pointed bill**. Best mark **vague dark line through eye**; male's dull-orange crown sometimes visible. Breeding form in Region **evenly yellow except for olive back**. Migratory northern form gray-headed, duller, **brightest yellow under tail**.

Similar Species: Yellow Warbler (page 301) plain-faced, bill larger. Female Wilson's Warbler (page 315) shows vague dark cap, often flits tail. MacGillivray's Warbler (page 311) with more distinct hood. Nashville Warbler (page 299) has prominent eye-ring.

Seasonal Abundance: Common summer resident in Region, rare in winter. Migrants return by late March; fall migration protracted, can continue into November. Breeds across Canada, south in western U.S. to Mexican border; winters Pacific Coast, southeastern U.S., Mexico south to El Salvador.

Where to Find: Breeds throughout Region, away from cities, to tree line. Migrants can be anywhere. In winter, dense, overgrown thickets, hedgerows.

Habitat: Brushy forest edge including regenerating clearcuts. Blackberry thickets preferred in winter.

Diet and Behavior: Forages relatively low on insects, some fruit. Also feeds on nectar. Joins mixed-species flocks in migration.

Voice: Song colorless trill that drops off at end. Call high, sharp chip.

Did you know? Orange-crowned Warblers sometimes feed at sapsucker wells in winter.

Date and Location Seen: _____

Description: 4½". Agile warbler, **bright-yellow below to throat**, variably whitish on belly. **Gray head**, greenish **plain wings**, prominent **white eye-ring**. MALE: Brighter with vague rust crown patch. Both sexes duller in fall.

Similar Species: Female Yellow Warbler (page 301) shows weak eye-ring but lacks grayish head. MacGillivray's Warbler (page 311) has grayish throat, white crescents above, below eye.

Seasonal Abundance: Common migrant in Region (especially at higher elevations), fairly common summer resident, mid-April–August. Breeds in forest zones across southern Canada, northern U.S., south in Appalachians, Pacific Coast states; winters south to Guatemala.

Where to Find: Breeds southern foothills, mountains, sparsely to Columbia Gorge, rarely Coast Range. Migrants widespread.

Habitat: Sunny, dry brushlands, hillsides; open woodlands with heavy underbrush. Attracted to *Ceanothus*-covered slopes.

Diet and Behavior: Forages for insects mostly low, often in outer branches, shifting tail while actively flitting through foliage. Joins mixed flocks during spring migration, may feed higher in canopy. Nests on ground in dense growth.

Voice: Slow, sweet, two-part song, *wee tsee, wee tsee, wee tsee, chiddle chiddle chiddle*. Call note sharp chip.

Did you know? Alexander Wilson discovered this warbler on migration near Nashville, Tennessee, and named it after the city.

Date and Location Seen: _____

Male

Female

YELLOW WARBLER
Dendroica petechia

Description: 4¾". Short-tailed, **all-yellow**, darker above; wings with lighter feather edges. **Dark eye prominent on plain face**. Yellow tail spots. MALE: Bright-yellow with distinct **reddish-brown breast streaks**. FEMALE: Duller, no breast streaks; can show **indistinct yellow eye-ring**.

Similar Species: Wilson's Warbler (page 315) female with longer tail, hint of dark cap. Orange-crowned Warbler (page 297) with dark line through eye. Nashville Warbler (page 299) with gray head, strong eye-ring. Common Yellowthroat (page 313) female with gray-white belly.

Seasonal Abundance: Common resident in Region, May–September. Spring migrants continue to pass through into June; fall movement begins in July. Breeds across North America (except Gulf Coast, Mojave Desert) south to South America. North American breeders winter from southern California, Mexico, West Indies to Amazonian Brazil.

Where to Find: Breeds throughout Region in appropriate habitat. Migrants more widespread.

Habitat: Near water in shrubby areas, woodland edge.

Diet and Behavior: Forages at various heights, primarily for insects, some fruit. Joins mixed flocks in migration.

Voice: Song *sweet sweet sweet I'm so sweet*. Call notes include thin *tsip*, loud chip.

Did you know? Brown-headed Cowbirds often lay eggs in Yellow Warbler nests. To foil them, the warblers sometimes build a new nest over the top of all the eggs and lay a fresh set.

Date and Location Seen: _____

Audubon's
Male Breeding

Non-breeding

Myrtle
Male Breeding

Description: 5¼". **Yellow on rump**, sides of breast; **white tail spots. Brown in winter with streaked breast**. Male in breeding plumage has small yellow crown patch (sometimes obscured), gray back, **black breast with sides streaked down to white belly**. Two distinct forms in Region. MYRTLE WARBLER: **White throat**, white wing-bars, **black mask**; female browner than male, lacks bib. AUDUBON'S WARBLER: **Yellow throat**, gray head, **solid white wing patch**; female browner than male with streaked breast, less yellow on throat. In winter, head plainer than Myrtle.

Similar Species: Distinctive in breeding plumage. In winter, separable from sparrows by thin bill, yellow rump.

Seasonal Abundance: AUDUBON'S common summer resident in Region; both forms common in migration, uncommon in winter. Breeds North America to Central America (MYRTLE in north, AUDUBON'S in West), winters south to West Indies, Panama.

Where to Find: Throughout Region.

Habitat: Breeds in coniferous forest, winters in agricultural areas, brushy woods.

Diet and Behavior: Forages for insects, berries among leaves, twigs; also flycatches. Fruit intake increases in winter (wax myrtle preferred). Flocks outside breeding season.

Voice: Variable, two-part song — clear, warbled trill, usually rising or falling at end. MYRTLE chip note loud *tup*, AUDUBON'S weaker *chwit*.

Did you know? The two forms have often been considered separate species.

Date and Location Seen: _____

Male

Female Immature

Description: 4¾″. **Black-and-white head pattern** with **small yellow spot in front of eye**; gray back, white wing-bars, **white underneath with dark side streaks**; white underside of tail. MALE: Black cap, cheek, extensive bib. FEMALE: Crown, cheek grayer, throat white with bib reduced (can be absent in immature).

Similar Species: Townsend's Warbler (page 307) with yellow on face, underparts.

Seasonal Abundance: Fairly common resident in Region, mid-April to September; a few linger later. Breeds southwestern British Columbia, Colorado south to northwestern Mexico, winters southern California, Texas south through central Mexico.

Where to Find: Throughout Region at lower elevations; seldom nests in urbanized areas. Migrants widespread.

Habitat: Breeds mostly in mixed conifer/oak woodlands in valley bottoms, alder, maple in foothills. Migrants use more-varied habitats.

Diet and Behavior: Forages for insects at various heights in canopy. Gleans, hovers, sallies for prey. Joins mixed-species flocks in migration.

Voice: Song variable, husky series of buzz notes with emphatic ending. Calls include low, dull chip.

Did you know? In the southern portion of their breeding range Black-throated Gray Warblers are closely associated with oak forests — quite different from their haunts of alder and maple woods with scattered conifers in the Pacific Northwest.

Date and Location Seen: _____

Male

Female

Description: 4¾". **Black-and-yellow head pattern, yellow breast with dark streaks at sides**, greenish back, white wing-bars, whitish belly. MALE: Black cap, cheek, bib, divided by bright-yellow. FEMALE: Crown, cheek lighter, bib reduced (absent in immature).

Similar Species: Black-throated Gray Warbler (page 305) lacks yellow except for dot in front of eye. Hermit Warbler (page 309) white below with yellow face, gray back.

Seasonal Abundance: In Region, uncommon summer resident at high elevations in Cascades; common migrant, uncommon winter resident in lowlands. Breeds Alaska to Idaho, winters southwestern British Columbia down coast to Mexico, Central America.

Where to Find: Widespread in migration. In winter, small numbers regular in cities, at bird feeders.

Habitat: Mature coniferous forest. Wintering birds often associate with cedars.

Diet and Behavior: Gleans, hover-gleans for insects high in canopy. Joins mixed-species flocks in migration, winter.

Voice: Buzzy song variable with several evenly-pitched notes followed by thin, high notes. Call quiet but sharp chip.

Did you know? Townsend's Warbler often hybridizes with Hermit Warbler where their breeding ranges overlap, resulting in intermediate forms.

Date and Location Seen: _____

Male

Female

Description: 4¾". **Black-throated**, white below with streaked **grayish back**, bold white **wing-bars, plain yellow face**. MALE: Black nape, **underparts clean-white**, sharp throat border. FEMALE: Duller, tinged buff, olive; cheek dusky, bib reduced (may be absent in immature).

Similar Species: Townsend's Warbler (page 307) with dark cheek patch, yellow-streaked breast, greenish back. Hybrid Townsend's × Hermit Warblers variable with mixed characters, often yellow-faced like Hermit but breast yellowish or streaked.

Seasonal Abundance: Fairly common resident in Region, late April–September; rarely winters. Breeds southwestern Washington to southern California, winters south to Central America.

Where to Find: Throughout at middle to high elevations; rare migrant in lowlands.

Habitat: Breeds in mature Douglas-fir, other coniferous forest. Migrants may use mixed woods, brush.

Diet and Behavior: Gleans, hover-gleans, flycatches, hangs upside down foraging for insects, spiders, usually in tops of large conifers. Later in season joins mixed flocks.

Voice: Variable song rapidly accelerating series of wheezy notes, less buzzy than Townsend's Warbler, ends with abrupt pitch change. Call quiet but sharp chip.

Did you know? Hermit Warbler nests in forests above the range of Black-throated Gray Warbler and below that of Townsend's Warbler. It is Oregon's most abundant warbler west of the Cascades.

Date and Location Seen: _____

Male

Description: 5″. Skulking warbler, **olive above** with **plain wings, gray hood, white crescents above, below eye, yellow lower breast, belly**. MALE: Hood bluish-gray. Blackish marks through eye, on bib. FEMALE: Duller, lacks blackish markings.

Similar Species: Gray-headed form of Orange-crowned Warbler (page 297) similar with less distinct hood, eye crescents. Nashville Warbler (page 299) lacks hood, has yellow throat, complete white eye-ring.

Seasonal Abundance: Fairly common in Region, mid-April to September. Migrants secretive. Breeds in western North America from southeastern Alaska to southwestern states, winters Mexico to Panama.

Where to Find: Locally from lowlands to near tree line. Most reliable at clearcuts in foothills.

Habitat: Forest edge with dense understory, including recent clearcuts, burns, brushy Scot's-broom-dominated fields.

Diet and Behavior: Forages under cover in dense, low growth for insects. Male sometimes sings from exposed, elevated perch. Pairs greet intruders with loud call notes.

Voice: Song rhythmic series of buzzy trills with last notes lower-pitched, slurred. Calls include loud, sharp *tsik*.

Did you know? MacGillivray's Warbler was first described by John James Audubon, who named it after the Scottish ornithologist William MacGillivray. The first specimens were taken near Vancouver, Washington, by J.K. Townsend, for whom Townsend's Warbler is named.

Date and Location Seen: _____

Male

Female

COMMON YELLOWTHROAT
Geothlypis trichas

Description: 4¾". Wren-like warbler, olive above with **plain wings, whitish-gray belly, yellow throat, breast, undertail**. MALE: **Black "bandit" mask** bordered by white above. FEMALE: Without mask, browner.

Similar Species: Other yellowish warblers lack mask, whitish-gray belly.

Seasonal Abundance: Common resident in Region, April–September; rarely lingers into winter. Breeds across Canada, Lower 48 states, winters south to West Indies, Panama.

Where to Find: Widespread throughout Region, loudly singing from most wetland habitats.

Habitat: Low, dense, wetland vegetation, but also uses brushy, Scot's-broom-dominated fields.

Diet and Behavior: Creeps through thick cover foraging for insects. Sometimes feeds on ground. Male sings from elevated perches.

Voice: Song whistled *witchety witchety witchety witchety*. Calls include often-given cheep, electric-like *bizz*.

Did you know? In courtship, male Common Yellowthroats perform a flight display in which they rise up to 100 feet in the air, calling and singing.

Date and Location Seen: _____

Male

Description: 4¾". **Yellow below**, brightest on plain face, **olive-green above, wings plain**. Frequent tail-, wing-flitting. MALE: **Round inky-black cap**. FEMALE: **Indistinct cap** makes yellow eyebrow stand out. IMMATURE: Lighter cap.

Similar Species: Yellow Warbler (page 301) female with shorter tail, lacks any trace of cap. Orange-crowned Warbler (page 297) with dark line through eye, thinner bill.

Seasonal Abundance: Common resident in Region, mid-April to mid-September. Extremely rare in winter. Breeds across northern North America, south in western mountains to northern New Mexico, central California. Winters Gulf Coast, Mexico south to Panama.

Where to Find: Throughout Region, but nesting uncommon in urban areas. Common migrant in all habitats.

Habitat: Nests in moist tangles, thickets near openings in deciduous or mixed woods, including regenerating clearcuts.

Diet and Behavior: Flits through foliage at various heights feeding mostly on insects. Sallies, gleans from small branches. Eats some berries. Sings constantly in spring.

Voice: Song emphatic series of slurred chips that builds in volume, speed. Call nasal *timp*, quite different from other warblers.

Did you know? Wilson's Warbler and four other American bird species are named for pioneering ornithologist Alexander Wilson.

Date and Location Seen: _____

Description: 7¼". Large, long-tailed, atypical warbler, **plain grayish-green wings**, back. **Bright-yellow breast**, throat; belly white to undertail. Dark cheeks, **white spectacles**, mustache mark; black line from eye to **stout black bill**.

Similar Species: Other warblers in Region smaller with thin bills; male Common Yellowthroat (page 313) has black mask.

Seasonal Abundance: Uncommon summer resident in Region, late April–September. Breeds southwestern Canada, mid-Atlantic states to central Mexico; winters Mexico to Panama.

Where to Find: Lowlands, lower foothills, mostly southwestern part of Region, becoming rare northward. Best bets: E.E. Wilson Wildlife Area, Fern Ridge Reservoir.

Habitat: Willow thickets, blackberry tangles, other dense deciduous growth, often in open woods beside ponds, streams.

Diet and Behavior: Skulks in thick cover, foraging mostly for insects, later in season for fruit. Shy, difficult to see except in spring when displaying male launches into short, contorted song-flights. Builds bulky, well-concealed nest near ground.

Voice: Sings loudly from tangles day or night, remarkable running assortment of squawks, rasping gurgles, rattles, whistles, interspersed with long pauses.

Did you know? To the naked eye, Yellow-breasted Chats exhibit only slight differences between males and females. However, breast color of the two sexes differs strongly in the ultraviolet spectrum, which is invisible to humans.

Date and Location Seen: _____

Male Breeding

Female

Description: 6¾". Compact, with **fairly stout bill**. MALE: Black back, tail, wings, **yellow-and-white wing-bars**. Adult **bright-yellow with scarlet head** in breeding plumage; immature, non-breeding-plumaged birds lack red on head. FEMALE: Lacks red head. Olive replaces black areas of male; back, belly can be gray. Wing-bars reduced but still conspicuous.

Similar Species: Female Bullock's Oriole (page 357) with much more pointed bill, orange in tail. Warblers smaller.

Seasonal Abundance: Common resident in Region, May–early September; uncommon into October. Breeds in West from northwestern Canada to Mexican border, winters Mexico to Costa Rica.

Where to Find: Throughout Region, but rarely nests successfully in urban areas. Easiest to spot at forest edges. Migrants can be inconspicuous in canopy.

Habitat: Fairly open coniferous or mixed forest; migrants use varied habitats.

Diet and Behavior: Gleans methodically in treetops, mostly for insects; occasionally sallies. Also takes fruit, especially in fall. Migrants often move in small flocks.

Voice: Song short series of slow phrases similar to that of American Robin, but hoarser. Call distinctive *pid er ick*.

Did you know? Tanagers are a New World group of over 200 species, most of which live in the tropics. Western Tanager is the northernmost of the four tanager species that occur regularly in the United States.

Date and Location Seen: _____

Male

Juvenile

Description: 7¾". **Dark hood**, upper body contrast with **rufous sides, white belly. Bold white spots on back, white outer corners on black tail**. Dark conical bill, red eye. Male black, female grayer. JUVENILE: Heavily streaked, lacks hood.

Similar Species: Dark-eyed Junco (page 341) smaller, bill pinkish, entire tail edge white, lacks white back spots. Smaller size, lack of white tail corners separate streaked sparrows from juvenile towhee.

Seasonal Abundance: Common resident in Region except at higher elevations in winter. Ranges from southern British Columbia throughout western North America to Guatemala; northern interior birds move south in winter.

Where to Find: Throughout Region, primarily lowlands; also mountains, but absent from closed-canopy forests. Thrives in urban areas, nesting in backyards.

Habitat: Open woods with dense, shrubby understory; thickets, overgrown fields.

Diet and Behavior: Forages mostly on ground for seeds, insects, fruits. Recorded taking lizards, other small vertebrates. Scratches ground vigorously with both feet while feeding. Does not flock, although found with other sparrows. Eats spilled grain on ground below bird feeders.

Voice: Song variable, buzzy trill. Call, given often, rising *schreeee*.

Did you know? The Spotted Towhee is quite variable throughout its large range. It and the closely related Eastern Towhee were long treated as a single species, the Rufous-sided Towhee.

Date and Location Seen: _____

Breeding

Juvenile

Description: 5¼". **Slim**, fairly long-tailed sparrow with streaked back, **unstreaked gray breast**. BREEDING: **Rufous cap bordered by white eyebrow**, black line through eye. NON-BREEDING: Browner; cap dull, streaked. JUVENILE: Resembles non-breeding but with streaked breast, pinkish bill.

Similar Species: Other small sparrows in Region shorter-tailed, less slim-appearing. American Tree Sparrow (not shown; rare winter resident in Region) similar but with central breast spot, less distinct rufous eye-line.

Seasonal Abundance: Fairly common summer resident in Region, mid-April–September; extremely rare in lowlands in winter. Breeds across continent from central Alaska, Newfoundland, south through U.S., in mountains to Nicaragua. Winters southern U.S., Mexico southward through breeding range.

Where to Find: Open forests, clearcuts in mountains; low-elevation woodlands, orchards.

Habitat: Open woods, woodland edge with grassy areas.

Diet and Behavior: Forages mostly on ground for seeds, insects. Seldom observed in flocks in Region. Sometimes sallies for flying insects.

Voice: Song mechanical-sounding long trill, all on one pitch. Calls include sharp chip, thin *seet*.

Did you know? Chipping Sparrows make use of animal hair in building their nests. Woven hair makes up the bulk of the nest in some cases.

Date and Location Seen: _____

Description: 6″. Long-tailed, grayish-brown sparrow streaked above, sparsely below, with chestnut shoulder patch (difficult to see), prominently **white-edged tail**. Bill, legs pinkish. Face pattern distinctive; thin **white eye-ring, light-centered ear patch with dark edge, bordered by light cheek**.

Similar Species: Juvenile Dark-eyed Junco (page 341) browner, face plain. Savannah Sparrow (page 327) may show lighter outer tail, but shorter, notched; head stripes prominent.

Seasonal Abundance: Uncommon migrant, summer resident in Region (mid-March–September); very rare in winter. Ranges across Canada, most of U.S., winters southern U.S. to Mexico.

Where to Find: Lowlands, foothills, mostly in southern part of Region, rare farther north; extirpated as breeder in southwestern Washington.

Habitat: Fields, pastures, fencerows with open ground, low grass, scattered shrubs; weedy Christmas-tree farms.

Diet and Behavior: Forages on ground for insects, seeds, by walking or running. Nests on ground. Male sings from exposed, elevated perch. Forms flocks, especially in migration; may fly to trees when flushed.

Voice: Musical song two long whistles, then series of jumbled trills. Calls include sharp chip, rising *seeet*.

Did you know? The subspecies of Vesper Sparrow living west of the Cascades has declined precipitously due to changes in land-use practices.

Date and Location Seen: _____

Description: 5¼". **Small, streaked below**, above. **Short notched tail**, whitish central crown stripe, **yellowish eyebrow**, pinkish bill, legs. Eyebrow yellower in spring, summer.

Similar Species: Song Sparrow (page 331) larger; richer brown with dense, thick streaks on breast. Lincoln's Sparrow (page 333) gray-headed with buff mustache mark, finer breast streaks. Vesper Sparrow (page 325) has longer, white-edged tail, lacks crown stripe.

Seasonal Abundance: Common migrant, summer resident in Region, uncommon in winter.

Where to Find: Open grasslands in summer; with other sparrows in hedges, berry tangles in winter. Migrants may appear anywhere, even in cities.

Habitat: Open grassland, agricultural fields, associated edges.

Diet and Behavior: Forages mostly on ground for insects, seeds. Forms flocks, especially in migration, winter. Male sings from elevated perches.

Voice: Buzzy song of 2–3 longer notes followed by lower-pitched, less clear buzzes. Calls include sharp, high, but quiet *pik*, thin *tsew*.

Did you know? There is considerable variation in the plumages of the many races of Savannah Sparrow that migrate through the Willamette Valley Region. Birds that winter are usually not those that summer.

Date and Location Seen: _____

Sooty

Gray-headed

Description: 6¼". Bulky, **plain-faced sparrow with chevron-shaped spots** on whitish breast, reddish-brown tail, pale lower bill. Two types in Region. SOOTY: Variably **dark-chocolate-brown** to gray-brown with **dense markings below**. GRAY-HEADED: **Gray on head, back**, contrasting with rusty wings.

Similar Species: Song Sparrow (page 331) has gray eyebrow. Hermit Thrush (page 283) has thin bill.

Seasonal Abundance: SOOTY: Common migrant, winter resident in Region, early September–early May. Breeds coastally Alaska to Washington, winters to California. GRAY-HEADED: Fairly common summer resident in Region near subalpine zone in Cascades; rare in lowlands. Breeds mountains of northwestern North America, winters south to California.

Where to find: SOOTY: Throughout Region at lower elevations. GRAY-HEADED: Clearcuts, open brush fields on west slopes of Cascades, mainly Santiam Pass southward.

Habitat: Mountain breeding habitat dry brushy areas with small trees; winter birds in hedges, berry tangles. Migrants widespread.

Diet and Behavior: Forages mostly on ground for seeds, insects, some fruit. Scrapes ground with both feet, jumping forward, kicking back. Sings fall, spring in lowlands. Visits feeders.

Voice: Song rich, complex, melodic, staccato, lively. Calls include hard, smacking *chink*.

Did you know? The Fox Sparrow is bewilderingly variable across its continent-wide range. While Sooty and Gray-headed types are separable in the field, each actually comprises several confusing geographic races.

Date and Location Seen: _____

Description: 6″. Streaked brownish above with brown wings. **Dark, dense streaking** may merge into central spot on whitish breast. **Long, rounded tail pumped in flight. Wide gray eyebrow**, brown crown with gray central stripe, dark mustache mark. JUVENILE: Buffier below.

Similar Species: Fox Sparrow (page 329) lacks broad eyebrow. Savannah (page 327), Lincoln's (page 333) Sparrows more trim-appearing. Swamp Sparrow (not shown; rare winter resident in Region) plain gray below.

Seasonal Abundance: Common resident in Region. Ranges across North America, south to northern Mexico.

Where to Find: Most abundant sparrow in Region; found throughout, up to mountain passes.

Habitat: Prefers shrubs, thicket edge in wetter areas, but frequents all semi-open habitats, broken forest.

Diet and Behavior: Feeds mostly on ground on insects, seeds (including below bird feeders), some fruit. Less prone to flock but can be gregarious in migration. Sings year round; in Region, begins nesting in late winter.

Voice: Song begins with several clear notes followed by lower note, jumbled trill. Calls include distinctive nasal *chump*, thin *seet*.

Did you know? Over 30 subspecies of this highly variable sparrow have been recognized. Song Sparrows resident in the Willamette Valley Region are among the darkest. In migration and winter they are joined by other races, including a few lighter-colored birds.

Date and Location Seen: _____

Description: 5¼". **Small**, secretive. Streaked above, below. **Buff wash on breast with distinct fine, dark streaks that end abruptly** at clear white belly. Short tail, small bill, grayish face with divided brown crown, **buff mustache mark**, faint eye-ring.

Similar Species: Smaller than Song Sparrow (page 331), with finer streaks. Lacks white or yellow eyebrow of Savannah Sparrow (page 327).

Seasonal Abundance: Common migrant, fairly common in winter at lower elevations in Region. Fairly common breeder in Cascades, April–September. Breeds from Alaska across Canada, south in western mountains; winters U.S. coasts, West Indies, south through Middle America.

Where to Find: Widespread in lowlands in winter, scarce in developed areas. In summer, mid- to high-elevation wetlands in Cascades.

Habitat: Breeds in open meadows, bogs. Prefers wet, scrubby places at all seasons, but migrants use variety of habitats.

Diet and Behavior: Feeds mostly on ground on seeds, insects, in or near cover. Less often in groups, but flocks with other sparrows.

Voice: Song fairly long series of bubbly musical trills, notes, generally given only on nesting grounds. Call sharp but soft chip.

Did you know? In fall, Lincoln's Sparrows often associate with other sparrows in wet fields; in spring, they may keep company with warblers in drier sites.

Date and Location Seen: _____

White-striped form

Tan-striped form

Description: 6¼". Colorful sparrow with **unstreaked gray breast**, light-and-dark head stripes, **bright-white throat**, buff-streaked back, **rusty wings** with white wing-bars. May have either tan or white head stripes; white-striped form has yellow spot between eye, bill. IMMATURE: Duller plumage with streaked breast.

Similar Species: White-crowned (page 337), Golden-crowned (page 339) Sparrows larger, grayer, throats dull-grayish, backs lack rich color tones. Swamp Sparrow (not shown; rare winter resident in Region) with grayer head, no wing-bars.

Seasonal Abundance: Uncommon, increasing migrant, winter resident in Region (late September–May). Breeds across Canada to Massachusetts, New York, winters to southern states.

Where to Find: Mostly lowlands throughout Region.

Habitat: Woodland edge, thickets, hedgerows, neighborhoods.

Diet and Behavior: Eats seeds, waste grain, insects, berries. Flocks with other sparrows, especially Golden-crowned, feeding on open ground; dives into dense cover when disturbed. Feeds below bird feeders, scratching with both feet.

Voice: Whistled song begins with two short notes followed by three long, quavering notes, all on same pitch. Call sharp, distinctive *chink* or high, thin *seet*.

Did you know? Recent breeding-population expansion of White-throated Sparrows in British Columbia has been reflected by higher wintering numbers on the West Coast.

Date and Location Seen: _____

Breeding

Immature

WHITE-CROWNED SPARROW
Zonotrichia leucophrys

Description: 6½". Fairly large, long-tailed, with **unstreaked gray breast, black-and-white head stripes, yellowish-orange bill**. Faint white wing-bars, streaked back. IMMATURE: **Brown-and-gray head stripes**. JUVENILE: Streaked breast in summer.

Similar Species: White-throated Sparrow (page 335) browner, smaller, with clearly marked bright-white throat. Golden-crowned Sparrow (page 339) has dusky bill, immature with less defined head stripes.

Seasonal Abundance: Common summer resident in Region, less common in winter. Breeds across northern North America, south to California in West; winters Pacific Coast, western, central U.S., to Caribbean, Mexico.

Where to Find: Nests throughout Region up to mountain passes, including cities. Winters locally in lowlands, mostly in agricultural areas.

Habitat: Shrubby woodland edge, parks, cities. Farms, hedgerows preferred in winter.

Diet and Behavior: Forages mostly on ground for insects, seeds, other plant material. Occasionally flycatches from trees, bushes. Flocks with other sparrows.

Voice: Song begins with 1–2 whistled calls followed by rhythmic series of buzzy trilled notes. Calls include sharp *bink*, high, thin *seet*.

Did you know? Many of the White-crowned Sparrows that breed in the Willamette Valley move south for the winter, but others remain year round. They are joined in migration and winter by birds of a different, northern-breeding race.

Date and Location Seen: _____

Breeding

Immature

Description: 6¾". **Large, with unstreaked gray breast**, long tail, relatively small **dusky bill**. Streaked brown above with **two white wing-bars**. BREEDING: **Golden crown bordered by black cap**. NON-BREEDING: Lacks black, has only hint of gold. IMMATURE: Resembles non-breeding.

Similar Species: White-crowned Sparrow (page 337) appears grayer, with orange-pink bill. Adult has black-and-white head stripes (brown-and-buff in immature).

Seasonal Abundance: Common winter resident in Region. Arrives mid-September, departs by mid-May. Breeds from Alaska south through British Columbia to U.S. border. Winters along coast from just north of Washington to northern Baja California.

Where to Find: In winter, lower elevations throughout Region. Migrants also at high elevations.

Habitat: Brushy places, including neighborhoods.

Diet and Behavior: Forages on ground for seeds, insects, often in flocks with other sparrows. Also feeds in trees, shrubs on blossoms, buds, especially in spring. Occasionally flycatches from trees, bushes.

Voice: Song, often given in migration, series of several long, raspy, whistled notes. Call notes include thin *seep*, rich, loud *bink*.

Did you know? Golden-crowned Sparrows wander regularly as far as the East Coast.

Date and Location Seen: _____

Oregon
Male

Oregon
Female

Slate-colored
Male

Juvenile

Description: 5¾". Sparrow-shaped. Short, **pink conical bill, white outer tail feathers**, whitish belly. Two distinct forms in Region. OREGON JUNCO: Male with **black hood**, plain brown back; female duller with gray hood. SLATE-COLORED JUNCO: Completely **grayish** with white belly.

Similar Species: Vesper Sparrow (page 325) streaked above, below, lacks hood; other sparrows in Region lack white outer tail feathers. Juvenile juncos streaked above, below, can be mistaken for sparrow but have white tail edges, pinkish bill.

Seasonal Abundance: Common resident in Region; numbers increase in lowlands in winter. OREGON: Common year round (breeds, winters in West); SLATE-COLORED: Small numbers appear in winter (breeds northern forests, winters throughout Lower 48 states).

Where to Find: Throughout Region; nests uncommonly in suburban areas.

Habitat: Nests in coniferous, mixed woods, particular at brushy edges. In migration, winter can appear anywhere, including cities.

Diet and Behavior: Flocks forage on ground, also in trees, mostly for seeds, insects. Often scratches at ground with feet. Regular beneath bird feeders.

Voice: Trilled song similar to that of Chipping Sparrow but more musical. Most common call sharp *tsip*.

Did you know? Oregon and Slate-colored are just two of the many distinctive regional forms of the widely distributed, highly variable Dark-eyed Junco.

Date and Location Seen: _____

Male

Female

BLACK-HEADED GROSBEAK
Pheucticus melanocephalus

Description: 7¾". Larger than most finches. **Plump**, square-tailed, with **large conical bill**. MALE: Adult with black head, tail, wings. **Wings, tail with bold white marks**. Breast, rump tawny-brown. Immature without black head. FEMALE: Brown with little white in wings, tail. Strong **white head stripe, eyebrow, mustache mark**.

Similar Species: Evening Grosbeak (page 371) male with yellow eyebrow, female with plain head.

Seasonal Abundance: Common summer resident in Region. Migrants (often seen in cities) arrive in mid-April, first fall transients late July. Breeds in West, from southern British Columbia south through mountains of Mexico; winters Mexico.

Where to Find: Throughout Region up to mountain passes.

Habitat: Nests mostly in mature deciduous or mixed forests away from urban areas, but in migration more widespread.

Diet and Behavior: Insects, seeds, berries. Forages in trees. Occasional at bird feeders.

Voice: Melodious song long, whistled warble likened to "drunken robin". Distinctive call note, sharp *pik*, often reveals its presence.

Did you know? Both the male and the female Black-headed Grosbeak sing, which is not uncommon among finch-like birds.

Date and Location Seen: _____

Male

Female

Description: 5½". Compact, relatively long-tailed songbird, **white wing bars**, grayish, conical bill. MALE: Attractive. **Bright-blue upperparts**, throat; rusty breast; white below to undertail. FEMALE: **Unstreaked plain brownish** above, lighter buff below, variably blue on wings, rump. IMMATURE: Duller in respective sexes; young juvenile has streaky breast.

Similar Species: Male Western Bluebird (page 279) larger with thin bill, lacks wing-bars. Small finches, sparrows streaked above.

Seasonal Abundance: Fairly common in southern, uncommon in northern parts of Region, May–September. Ranges across West from southern Canada, winters to Mexico.

Where to Find: Throughout Region to mountain passes.

Habitat: Meadows, shrubby grasslands, alpine openings, Christmas-tree farms; migrants use roadsides, weedy fields.

Diet and Behavior: Forages on ground, low brush for insects, seeds. Males sing persistently from fairly high perches, remaining immobile in foliage, hence sometimes difficult to spot. Nests low in thickets where females remain less visible. Forms small flocks in late summer.

Voice: Best located by song, lively jumble of warbled notes similar to that of Yellow Warbler (page 301). Call thin, sharp *pik*.

Did you know? The name lazuli comes from lapis lazuli, a semi-precious stone of a brilliant shade of blue. Finely ground, this mineral produces ultramarine — a rare and costly pigment in the artist's palette.

Date and Location Seen: _____

Male

Female

Description: 8¾". Medium-sized blackbird with fairly s**tout, pointed bill.** MALE: **Glossy-black with red shoulder patch** bordered with yellow-buff. FEMALE: Smaller; dark-brown above, **heavily streaked** below with strong **buff eyebrow**.

Similar Species: Tricolored Blackbird (not shown; uncommon, local in Region) male's shoulder patch bordered white, not yellow; female with darker belly, grayer throat.

Seasonal Abundance: Common resident in Region. In winter shifts from marshes to farms, retreats from higher altitudes. Breeds across continent south of subarctic zone to Bahamas, Central America; leaves northern areas in winter.

Where to Find: Nests throughout Region up to mountain passes in suitable habitat. In winter roosts in wetlands but feeds more in agricultural areas.

Habitat: Marshes, meadows, brushy edge. Farms, feedlots in winter.

Diet and Behavior: Seeds, insects. Forages mostly on ground but sometimes in trees. Flocks with other blackbirds. Often at bird feeders. During nesting, polygamous males protect territory with frequent song, aggressively chasing out intruders.

Voice: Main song of male *conk a ree*. Calls include *chek* note, rattles.

Did you know? Red-winged Blackbirds give more than 20 different vocalizations, a reflection of their complex social organization. Males have 18 different calls, females six. Four alarm calls are given by both sexes.

Date and Location Seen: _____

Description: 9". Heavy-bodied, **short-tailed** member of blackbird family. Back, sides streaked brown. **Bright-yellow underparts** with V-shaped black breast band. **Outer tail feathers white.** In flight, weak flapping alternates with gliding.

Similar Species: European Starling (page 291) lacks yellow underparts, white outer tail feathers.

Seasonal Abundance: Locally fairly common summer resident in Region, common in winter. Breeds from southern British Columbia to Michigan, south through Mexican highlands; winters from all but northernmost part of breeding range south to Gulf states, Mexico.

Where to Find: Widespread in winter. In summer, most reliable Albany to Eugene. Nearly extirpated as breeder in interior southwestern Washington.

Habitat: Fields, prairies, farms.

Diet and Behavior: Feeds on ground for insects, seeds. Probes soil with long, pointed bill. In winter usually in flocks. Often perches, sings high in trees, even during migration, winter; also sings from ground.

Voice: Song gurgling series of flute-like notes. Calls include *chupp*, rattle, thin, high buzz in flight.

Did you know? The Western Meadowlark is visually almost identical to the Eastern Meadowlark. Noting its different song, John James Audubon recognized that Western Meadowlark was a different species. He named it *neglecta* in Latin because others had overlooked it.

Date and Location Seen: _____

Male

Female

Description: 9½". **Large, stout-billed**, with **yellow head**, breast, lower belly. MALE: Black body, wings, behind bill; yellow parts bright, orange-tinged on head; **white patch on wing**. Immature duller. FEMALE: **Smaller**, browner; yellow areas dull; cheeks dusky. JUVENILE: Pale overall with buff feather edges.

Similar Species: Other blackbirds lack yellow on head, breast.

Seasonal Abundance: Uncommon resident in Region, April–September; rare in winter. Breeds in western North America, southern Canada to Great Lakes states; winters south to Mexico.

Where to Find: Local. Good spots include Fern Ridge Reservoir, Sauvie Island, Ridgefield National Wildlife Refuge. Migrants mix with other blackbirds at farms.

Habitat: Bulrush, cattail marsh; brushy edges. Forages at farm fields, feedlots, occasionally bird feeders in migration, winter.

Diet and Behavior: Forages mostly on ground, low brush for seeds, insects. Gregarious; flocks with other blackbirds. Polygamous males arrive first in spring, establish territory, attract up to six females with frequent song, defending against other males of their kind as well as intruders of other species. Nests colonially in marsh vegetation, usually over fairly deep water.

Voice: Song variable, raucous, combining unmusical croaks, long buzzes. Calls include rattles, *kecks*.

Did you know? Yellow-headeds are dominant over Red-winged Blackbirds, chasing them from established territories.

Date and Location Seen: _____

Male

Female

Description: 9". Medium-sized blackbird with s**hort, pointed bill**, fairly long, rounded tail. MALE: **Glossy-blackish-green with purplish-iridescent head, light-yellow eye**. FEMALE: **Drab** gray-brown with dark eye.

Similar Species: Red-winged Blackbird (page 347) not as plain; female streaked, male with shoulder patch. Brown-headed Cowbird (page 355) smaller, bill more finch-like.

Seasonal Abundance: Common resident in Region, but local. Breeds across much of West, upper Midwest, south to California; winters in warmer parts of breeding range, southern Great Plains, western Gulf Coast states, Mexico.

Where to Find: Patchily distributed around cities; much easier to find in agricultural areas.

Habitat: Pastures, feed lots, roadsides, urban parking lots, other open places.

Diet and Behavior: Mostly insects, seeds; also waste grain, crumbs. Forages mostly on ground, often in flocks — sometimes with other blackbirds, starlings. Visits bird feeders.

Voice: Courting male has *kseee* call. Year-round nasal *check* note.

Did you know? Nest-site selection by Brewer's Blackbirds varies greatly depending on local availability. They may build their nests in trees, on plant stalks over water, in low shrubs, on the ground in high grass, or even on rocky ledges.

Date and Location Seen: _____

353

Male

Female

Juvenile

BROWN-HEADED COWBIRD
Molothrus ater

Description: 7½". Small blackbird with **stubby conical bill**, relatively **short, square-tipped tail**. MALE: Black with **brown head**. FEMALE: Smaller, **plain** gray-brown, lighter below, with vague streaks. JUVENILE: Similar to female but paler, streaking more distinct.

Similar Species: Short bill, brown head distinguish male from other blackbirds. Female smaller than blackbirds, plainer than sparrows.

Seasonal Abundance: Common summer resident in Region, most depart in winter. Breeds across North America from southern Yukon, Newfoundland, south through central Mexico; winters Midwest, southern states, Mexico.

Where to Find: Throughout Region, including cities.

Habitat: Widespread in breeding season in woodlands, neighborhoods, open areas. In migration prefers fields, farms.

Diet and Behavior: Feeds on ground, mostly on seeds, insects. Does not build nest, instead lays eggs in other birds' nests. In breeding season groups of males display with odd postures, spread wings, noisily chase females. Flocks with other blackbirds after breeding.

Voice: Male gives gurgling squeaks in display. Female rattles. Flight call thin, high whistle. Juveniles beg from host species with *cheep*, given frequently.

Did you know? Brown-headed Cowbirds, once restricted to plains habitats, invaded more-forested regions as land was cleared for agriculture, settlement, and lumber production. Cowbird nest parasitism is now implicated in the decline of many forest songbirds.

Date and Location Seen: _____

Male

Male Immature

Female

Description: 8". **Slim** with long tail, **tapered, pointed bill**. ADULT: Male **orange** with black cap, back, wings, eye-line, narrow bib, center of tail. **Large white wing patch**. Female duller, mostly gray-olive with whitish belly, **white wing-bars, orange wash on head, throat**. IMMATURE: Like female; male brighter with black throat.

Similar Species: Male unmistakable in Region. Female Western Tanager (page 319) with heavier, blunter bill, lacks orange tones. Size, bill shape distinguish from warblers, goldfinches.

Seasonal Abundance: Uncommon summer resident in Region. Arrives May, most depart by early August. Breeds southwestern Canada to Mexico, winters Mexico, Guatemala.

Where to Find: Mostly limited to low-elevation river edge, but also open groves, parks, suburban neighborhoods. Good bets include Sauvie Island oak groves, woodlands around Eugene.

Habitat: Prefers deciduous or mixed woodlands with large shade trees, especially cottonwoods along rivers.

Diet and Behavior: Forages in foliage of trees, bushes for insects, fruits, nectar from flowers. Weaves hanging bag-shaped nest in outer limbs, concealed by leaves but obvious in winter. Sometimes visits hummingbird feeders.

Voice: Series of rich, medium-pitched whistles, chatter. Calls include harsh *cshek*, rolling chatter.

Did you know? American orioles such as Bullock's are actually blackbirds — a New World family. Early naturalists gave them that name because they superficially resemble the Golden Oriole of Europe, a member of an unrelated family.

Date and Location Seen: _____

357

Male

Female

Description: 5¾". Stocky finch with **short, notched tail, stout bill**. MALE: **Raspberry-red** on head, breast, extending to flanks, infusing brown back. Adult **without streaks on belly**. FEMALE: Brownish without red. Blurry streaks on whitish-buff breast, belly. **Broad white eyebrow**.

Similar Species: House Finch (page 361) slimmer, male more orange-red with streaks on belly. Female lacks broad white eyebrow. Cassin's Finch (not shown; fairly common resident in eastern Oregon, reaches Region at Cascade crest, rare visitor to lowlands) has crisp, fine belly streaks.

Seasonal Abundance: Locally fairly common resident, migrant in Region. Transients appear in urbanized areas late April–early May. Breeds across continent in northern forests, south in Appalachians, Pacific coastal mountains. Winters eastern U.S., Pacific Coast states to Baja California.

Where to Find: Throughout rural, semi-rural parts of Region. Uncommon in cities, avoids dense forests.

Habitat: Mixed woods, coniferous forest edge, semi-open areas with fruiting trees.

Diet and Behavior: Forages on fruits, seeds, buds, some insects, mostly in flocks, especially outside nesting season. More arboreal than House Finch, but also feeds on ground. Uses bird feeders.

Voice: Series of warbled notes without harsh ending of House Finch song. Calls include muffled whistle, sharp *pik* given in flight.

Did you know? Purple Finches are declining in the Willamette Valley Region, probably due to habitat alterations.

Date and Location Seen: _____

Male

Female

Description: 5½". Sparrow-sized finch with long, only slightly notched tail. **Bill short, rounded.** MALE: Red (yellow in some individuals) on crown, breast, rump; **streaks on belly, flanks.** FEMALE: Brownish-gray without red. Blurry streaks on gray-white breast, belly. **No strong facial pattern.**

Similar Species: Purple Finch (page 359) more robust, adult male without streaks on lower breast, female with broad white eyebrow.

Seasonal Abundance: Common year-round resident in Region. Ranges from southern Canada south through Mexico.

Where to Find: Throughout Region, including cities, up to mountain passes.

Habitat: Urban neighborhoods, parks, suburbs, farms, woodland edge. Avoids dense forest.

Diet and Behavior: Often nests, feeds in backyards. Usually forages in flocks on ground, in weeds, or in trees for seeds, berries, blossoms, buds. Regular at sunflower feeders.

Voice: Series of cheery warbling notes often ending with harsh note. Call loud chirp.

Did you know? House Finches have benefited greatly from human development. Although fairly common over much of the West, including Oregon, when pioneers arrived, they did not move into the Willamette Valley until the 1940s. House Finches introduced to New York City in the 1940s have now spread throughout eastern North America.

Date and Location Seen: _____

Female

Male

RED CROSSBILL
Loxia curvirostra

Description: 6". Compact finch with **large head, short, notched tail**, plain dark wings. **Bill heavy with crossed tips**. MALE: Plumage variable; generally brick-red, sometimes orange, yellowish — brightest on crown, rump. FEMALE: Olive-yellow. JUVENILE: Dull, streaked.

Similar Species: Purple Finch (page 359), House Finch (page 361) smaller, less stubby, without crossed bill tips. Pine Grosbeak (not shown; rare in Region) larger with white wing-bars, uncrossed bill. White-winged Crossbill (not shown; rare in Region) with white wing-bars.

Seasonal Abundance: Fairly common resident in Region. Nests at any time of year. Movements occur through cities, generally April–May. Ranges world wide, mostly above equator.

Where to Find: Erratic, nomadic. Localities, abundance vary with cone crops.

Habitat: Coniferous forest, including pine, spruce, Douglas-fir. Also mixed woods.

Diet and Behavior: Flocks seek productive conifers, pry cones open, extract seeds. Also eats other seeds, buds, insects, minerals from ground. Occasional at bird feeders.

Voice: Song rapid series of hard chirps, warbles. *Kip kip* call given in flight.

Did you know? There are at least eight different forms of Red Crossbill in North America, varying in bill size and in subtleties of their call notes. Each may wander in search of the cone type that its bill is best adapted to open.

Date and Location Seen: _____

Description: 4¾". Small finch, upperparts streaked brownish, underparts buff-white with **well-defined, heavy, dark streaking**. Yellowish on wings, tail, not always visible on perched bird, but male's bold yellow wing stripe evident in flight. Tail notched. **Bill conical, long, pointed**.

Similar Species: Smaller than House Finch (page 361), Purple Finch (page 359); bill shape distinguishes from warblers, other finches. Common Redpoll (not shown; rare winter visitor in Region) has black chin, red cap.

Seasonal Abundance: Common resident in Region but can be scarce, local in late summer, fall. Breeds from Alaska across Canada, south through western U.S. to Guatemala; winters in all but northernmost part of breeding range, throughout U.S., Mexico.

Where to Find: Widespread in Region, usually near conifers. Migratory, nomadic; local abundance varies unpredictably.

Habitat: Coniferous forest, mixed woods (especially with alders), weedy areas.

Diet and Behavior: Gregarious. Feeds mostly in trees, but also on weed stalks, ground. Eats mostly seeds, but some insects taken. Large, compact flocks swirl noisily when alarmed. Flocks with other finches. Regular at thistle, black-oil sunflower seed feeders.

Voice: Song jumble of husky twitters, trills. Calls include rising *zreeee*, high, sharp *di di di*, both given in flight.

Did you know? In spring, Pine Siskins often glean insects from large limbs, feeding somewhat like a nuthatch.

Date and Location Seen: _____

Male

Female

Description: 4½". Small finch, **yellow from chin to undertail**, conical grayish bill, short, notched tail. MALE: **Black cap**; wings, back greenish; black **tail with extensive white patches**. Duller in winter. FEMALE: Duller, lacks cap; less white in wings, tail.

Similar Species: American Goldfinch (page 369) has white undertail; only forehead black, lacks white wing patch at base of flight feathers. Yellowish warblers have thin bills.

Seasonal Abundance: Year-round resident in Region, fairly common south, uncommon north, east; may wander in winter, withdraw from northern parts. Vagrant in western Washington. Ranges from southernmost central Washington (Klickitat County) throughout West to northern South America.

Where to Find: Mostly lowlands, rare into foothills.

Habitat: Fields, meadows, open areas with teasel, blackberry thickets, other weeds, brush; open oak woodlands.

Diet and Behavior: Feeds mostly on seeds from weed stalks, trees, shrubs, also on ground, rarely on insects; may frequent feeders in neighborhoods. Gregarious at all seasons; flocks with its own kind, also other small finches.

Voice: Twittering song less repetitive than that of American Goldfinch, may include mimicry of other birds. Calls include high, chimed *pee yeet*.

Did you know? Lesser Goldfinches from the eastern and southern parts of their range have black backs.

Date and Location Seen: _____

Male Breeding

Juvenile

Female Breeding

Description: 5″. Variable plumage with **prominent wing-bars**, white undertail. **Short, conical bill**, pinkish in summer. BREEDING: Male **bright-yellow** with black wings, forehead, tail. Female dull-yellow, olive on back, with **blackish wings**. NON-BREEDING: Dull with some yellow on throat. JUVENILE: Browner on back with buff wing-bars.

Similar Species: Lesser Goldfinch (page 367) with all-yellow underparts, more white in wings; male has black cap. Conical bill distinguishes from warblers; lack of streaks from sparrows, other finches.

Seasonal Abundance: Common resident in Region. Migratory; often difficult to find in winter. Breeds from southern Canada south to California, Oklahoma, Georgia; winters in all but northern fringe of breeding area, south through U.S. to Mexico.

Where to Find: Throughout Region; less common in cities.

Habitat: Farms, open deciduous woods, weedy lots, neighborhoods.

Diet and Behavior: Late nesting coincides with summer seed production. Eats small seeds on weed stalks, especially thistles; also in trees such as alder, birch, sometimes on ground. Favors thistle feeders in backyards.

Voice: Song long jumble of high, repeated twitters, phrases. Calls include *tee di di di*, mostly given in flight, thin *tweee*.

Did you know? In late summer, American Goldfinches flock in meadows to feed on dandelion and thistle seeds, then at bird feeders, before dispersing for the winter.

Date and Location Seen: _____

Male

Female

Description: 8". Plump, short-tailed finch with **massive conical bill**. Black wings, tail with **large white patches** on each. Bill green in spring, whitish in winter. MALE: **Bright-yellow eyebrow**. Dusky-brown head, chest grade to yellow belly, back. FEMALE: Brownish-gray with yellowish wash.

Similar Species: Black-headed Grosbeak (page 343) lacks yellow eyebrow of male, plain head of female. American Goldfinch (page 369) much smaller.

Seasonal Abundance: Fairly common in Region in summer, less common, irregular in winter. Easiest to find in May, even in cities. Ranges across southern Canada, south in western mountains to Mexico; some southward movement in winter.

Where to Find: Widespread. Especially conspicuous in lowlands in spring, e.g., Oregon State University campus (Corvallis).

Habitat: Primarily coniferous forest but also mixed woods.

Diet and Behavior: Gregarious outside breeding season. Large flocks may forage together, mostly in trees, on seeds, buds including maple, ash. Also eats insects, fruit, comes to ground for gravel. Regular at bird feeders (usually voracious).

Voice: Song repeated notes in series. Call strident, ringing *tcheew* given often by flocking birds.

Did you know? Their scientific and common names come from the erroneous notion that Evening Grosbeaks are most active after sunset, dating back to the first scientific description of the species in 1825.

Date and Location Seen: _____

Male

Female

Description: 6". An Old World sparrow, not closely related to native sparrows. **Chunky**, short-tailed, with **unstreaked** dingy-gray breast, brown-streaked upperparts. MALE: Gray crown, **black face, bib** with chestnut hind neck. Colors duller in winter. FEMALE: Plain, dull, with **light-buff eyebrow**.

Similar Species: Native sparrows not as compact. Finches of similar size streaked.

Seasonal Abundance: Common resident in Region. Introduced from Europe to North America, most of world.

Where to Find: Throughout Region, usually near human habitation.

Habitat: Cities, suburbs, farms.

Diet and Behavior: Feeds on ground, often in flocks, mostly on seeds, insects, crumbs. Noisily roosts in thick bushes. Competes aggressively for cavity nest sites, much to detriment of native species. Regular at bird feeders.

Voice: Repeated series of *chirrup* notes. Chirping call often given by many birds simultaneously, creating cheerful din. Also rattles in excitement.

Did you know? Male House Sparrows get brighter as they begin nesting, not as a result of molting, but through feather wear that reveals the attractive colors beneath.

Date and Location Seen: _____

Harlequin Duck
Male

Harlequin Duck
Female

Blue Grouse

Mountain Quail

HARLEQUIN DUCK
Histrionicus histrionicus

Small diving duck, nests beside rushing mountain streams, winters on rocky coasts. MALE: Darkly colored, mostly slate-blue with rusty sides, bold white marks on head, sides, back; dull as female in summer. FEMALE: Brown with white belly, white spot on cheek, another near bill base. In Region, uncommon summer resident in western Cascades.

BLUE GROUSE
Dendragapus obscurus

Large chicken-like bird of conifer forests. Tail with gray band at tip. Male (shown) upperparts mostly sooty-brown, underparts bluish-gray; female lighter, bluish tones muted. Now absent from most of lowlands in Region due to deforestation, but fairly common from foothills to mountain passes. Often detected by male's call, series of soft, low, far-carrying hoots, from perch high in tree.

MOUNTAIN QUAIL
Oreortyx pictus

Large, secretive quail of open, shrubby habitats. Brownish back, gray breast, chestnut flanks barred white, chestnut throat with white border, long, straight head plume. Uncommon, local year-round resident south of Columbia River in Region, mostly in foothills, slopes, ridges of Cascades, Coast Range. Forms flocks outside nesting season; often associated with early stages of regenerating clearcuts. Male's resonant yodel in spring carries great distance.

Northern Goshawk
Adult

Northern Goshawk
Immature

Northern Pygmy-Owl

Black-backed Woodpecker

NORTHERN GOSHAWK
Accipiter gentilis

Large, heavy-bodied, long-tailed forest hawk. Glides between short bursts of flapping. ADULT: Dark-gray above, light-gray beneath, with black cap, white eyebrow, black eye-line. IMMATURE: Larger version of Cooper's Hawk (page 103), heavily streaked beneath to undertail; bands on broad tail form wavy pattern when bird perched. Uncommon resident of older forest at higher elevations in Region; rare winter visitor in lowlands.

NORTHERN PYGMY-OWL
Glaucidium gnoma

Sparrow-sized, yellow-eyed, long-tailed owl of forests, woodland edges. Brownish upperparts, white belly with dark streaks. Small white spots on crown, sides; black false "eyes" on nape plumage. Active in daylight. Preys on small birds, mammals; presence often betrayed by noisy, mobbing songbirds. Fairly common but elusive resident in foothills, mountains of Region; in winter, sometimes seen in lowland woodlots, around towns, suburbs.

BLACK-BACKED WOODPECKER
Picoides arcticus

Black-and-white woodpecker of higher-elevation forests. Black back, white flanks barred with black, white mustache mark. Male (shown) has yellow crown patch. Uncommon to irregularly fairly common resident near Cascade crest in Region; concentrates opportunistically in recently burned or diseased timber stands to exploit insect infestations. Similar Three-toed Woodpecker (not shown; rare in Region in same habitats) has white back.

Gray Jay

Mountain Chickadee

Clark's Nutcracker

GRAY JAY
Perisoreus canadensis

Distinctive, small-billed jay of conifer forests. Adult (shown) has dark-gray upperparts, light-gray underparts. Dark cap set off by light forehead, cheeks. Juvenile overall dark-gray. Curious; begs from tourists, steals food in campgrounds. Often roams in family groups. Fairly common in intact, mid- to high-elevation conifer forest throughout Region, uncommon, local at lower elevations.

CLARK'S NUTCRACKER
Nucifraga columbiana

Distinctive relative of crows, jays, specialized for extracting seeds from pine cones. Medium-gray with long, black, pointed bill. Wings black with white patch on inner trailing edge conspicuous in flight. Tail black with white edges. Fairly common but local resident at higher elevations of Cascades; rare, irregular visitor elsewhere in Region. Pesters tourists, campers for handouts.

MOUNTAIN CHICKADEE
Poecile gambeli

Chickadee of relatively dry, open-canopy forests. Very similar to Black-capped Chickadee (page 253) but with white eyebrow, pale-gray flanks; wing feathers lack white edging. *Chick a dee* call hoarser, slower. Fairly common resident in Region at higher elevations of Cascades. Rare but regular visitor to lowlands in winter.

Mountain Bluebird Male

Mountain Bluebird Female

Townsend's Solitaire

Gray-crowned Rosy-Finc

MOUNTAIN BLUEBIRD
Sialia currucoides

Bluebird of dry, open country, parklands. MALE: All-blue, unmistakable in Region. FEMALE: Similar to Western Bluebird (page 279) but more slender with thinner bill, longer wings, tail; breast usually grayer but can be pale-orangish. Common summer resident in eastern Oregon. In Region, breeds locally along Cascade crest; rare winter visitor in lowlands.

TOWNSEND'S SOLITAIRE
Myadestes townsendi

Ground-nesting thrush of mid- to high-elevation forests. Slender, short-billed. Overall gray with prominent white eye-ring, white tail edges. Buffy wing stripe visible in flight, shows as small patch on folded wing. Fairly common but local summer resident in Region in open forests, clearcuts of Cascades, uncommonly in Coast Range. Uncommon spring migrant in lowlands; rare fall, winter.

GRAY-CROWNED ROSY-FINCH
Leucosticte tephrocotis

Chunky finch of high-mountain tundra. Bill fairly short, conical. Legs, feet black; bill yellow in winter, black in breeding season. Male (shown) mostly rich-brown with pinkish tones on belly, rump, wings. Throat, forehead dark, rest of head gray. Female, juvenile duller. In Region, fairly common year-round resident in high Cascades; breeds in remote, rocky clefts at edge of snowfields on alpine meadows. Rare visitor to lowlands, Coast Range in migration, winter.

Acknowledgments, Photographer Credits

Creating a bird identification guide is a significant undertaking and would not be possible without the contribution of many local birders. This book is based on *Birds of the Puget Sound Region* by Bob Morse, Tom Aversa, and Hal Opperman (R. W. Morse Company, 2003); we thank again all of the people who helped with that publication and whose names are listed there. In particular, we thank Bob Morse, who authored many of the introductory sections and several species accounts for the earlier book, for graciously allowing this material to reappear here. Thanks to Gina Calle for the design and layout of the book, Shawn K. Morse for the Willamette Valley Region map, Eric Kraig for the bird drawings, and Bob Wilson for his suggestions and encouragement.

We owe a great debt to the many photographers who have contributed to this book, consistently meeting the challenge of capturing a bird's key field marks in photographs of high technical and artistic merit. Their names are listed below. In particular, Lee Barnes, Jim Pruske, Robert Royse, Bart Rulon, Margaret St. Clair, and Brian Small spent countless hours going through their slide collections searching for just the right images for us. Special thanks to Tom Munson for permission to use his photo of an Acorn Woodpecker on the front cover and Sam Mann for the use of his Northern Pygmy-Owl photo on the back cover.

The letters following the page numbers refer to the position of the photograph on that page (T = top, B = bottom, L = left, R = right, N = inset).

Don Baccus: 80T. **Lee Barnes**: 42B, 46T, 50B, 54T, 58TR, 60B, 68, 92, 112, 116, 118, 130TL, 164, 172, 176, 180B, 216T, 248T, 260, 262, 300T, 378TL. **Tony Beck/VIREO**: 186N. **Brian Bell**: 28T, B, 30B, 196. **Rick and Nora Bowers**: 52T, 76N, 102T, 142TL, 166B, 210, 228, 302T. **Keith Brady**: 28N, 90, 128, 152T, 160B, 174, 242B, 254, 320T, 354BL, 358T, B, 370T, B, 378B. **Jane Cooper**: 96TR. **Mike Donahue**: 108N, 152B, 154T, B, 156B. **Mike Dossett**: 142BL. **Tom Eckert**: 66T, B, 100N, 134BR, 208, 212, 248B, 256T, 264, 284T, 306T, B, 326,

368N, 378TR. **James R. Gallagher/Sea & Sand Audubon**: 362. **Carrie Griffis**: 362N. **Sherry Hagen**: 100. **Gloria Hopkins**: 204. **Peter LaTourrette/VIREO**: 320B, 344T. **Kevin Li**: 240T, B. **Jerry Liguori**: 112N, 114T, 380BL. **Dan Logen**: 160T, 198L, R, 278T, B, 368T. **Gary Luhm**: 38T, 78, 126. **Stuart MacKay**: 96L, 124T, B, 136BR, 142BR, 146B, 374TL. **Sam Mann**: 376BL, back cover. **Mike McDowell**: 132T, 334T. **Dick McNeely**: 38N, 50N, 72B, 74B, 102B, 106B, 108T, 178N, 184B, 218T, 220, 234, 250, 292, 328T, 338B. **Tom Munson**: front cover, 102N, 110T, 194, 216B, 348. **Harry Nehls**: 156N, 324. **Olympic National Park**: 284B. **Dennis Paulson**: 182N, 234N. **Jim Pruske**: 26N, 58TL, BL, BR, 82, 88B, 96BR, 98N, 120, 130TR, 136T, 168, 170, 186, 202T, B, 232, 258, 290N, 294T, B, 336T, 338T, 340BR, 342T, B, 346B, 352B, 354T, BR, 356B, 368B, 372T, 374BL. **Jim Robertson**: 30T, 32T, 230, 302B, 340TR. **Jim Rosso**: 90N, 236N, 250N. **Robert Royse**: 26T, 38B, 42T, 44B, 54B, N, 56T, 64T, B, 130BL, BR, 132B, 138, 140T, B, 146T, 148TL, TR, B, 180T, 188B, 190B, 322T, 332, 334B, 340BL, 346T, 350T, 380TR. **Bart Rulon**: 32B, 34T, B, 36B, 56B, 70T, 78N, 88T, 136BL, 144, 252, 282, 286T, B, 330, 340TL, 360T, B, 372B, 374TR. **Margaret St. Clair**: 48T, 60T, 62T, 72T, 74T, 80N, 92N, 200L, 242T, 268, 276. **Michael Shepard**: 150T, N, 156T, 158T, N, 160N. **Brian Small**: 36T, 44T, 48B, 50T, 52B, 62B, 70B, 76T, B, 80B, 86, 94T, B, 104T, 110B, 134BL, 142TR, 150B, 158B, 162, 178, 184T, 192T, 196N, 200R, 202N, 206, 214, 218B, 222, 224, 226, 246, 256B, 266, 272, 280, 288, 290T, 296T, B, 298, 300B, 302N, 304T, B, 308T, B, 310, 312B, 314, 316, 318T, B, 322B, 328B, 336B, 344B, 350B, 352T, 356N, 364, 366T, B, 374BR, 376BR. **Ruth Sullivan**: 188T, 238N. **Brent Trim**: 236. **Idie Ulsh**: 166T. **Barry Wahl**: 40T, B, 84, 244, 270, 274, 290B, 312T, 380TL. **Brian Wheeler**: 98T, B, 104B, 106T, 108B, 110N, 114B, 122, 182, 376TL, TR. **John Williams**: 238. **Cathy Wise**: 356T. **Jim Zipp**: 192B, 380BR. **William Zittrich**: 190T. **Tim Zurowski**: 46B, 134T.

The success of this guide is the success of all those who have contributed to it. Their participation is sincerely appreciated.

Index/Checklist of Willamette Valley Birds

Use this checklist to keep a record of the birds you have seen. **Bold** numbers are for the main Species Account page.

387

Other Species Seen

_____

_____

_____

_____

_____

_____

_____

About the Authors

HARRY NEHLS

Has birded the Willamette Valley since 1949. He lectures and writes about birds for the Audubon Society of Portland, has authored three books, and serves as Secretary of the Oregon Record Committee and subregional editor for *North American Birds*.

TOM AVERSA

Co-author of *Birds of the Puget Sound Region*, records compiler for the Washington Ornithological Society, and member of the Washington Bird Records Committee, has worked at Woodland Park Zoo in Seattle since arriving from Massachusetts in 1996.

HAL OPPERMAN

Principal author of *A Birder's Guide to Washington* (American Birding Association) and co-author of *Birds of the Puget Sound Region*, has lived in the Seattle area since 1967. He is past editor of the Washington Ornithological Society's journal, *Washington Birds*.